Nicole—

Matt 11:28-30

JUST *Rest*

[signature]

"Sonja Corbitt uses interpretations of quantum mechanics to provide a solid base for advice on how to engage with Catholic spirituality and to help us see how the science fits into our picture of the world. Often when I read a book I like very much, I think, *I wish I had written that*. I'm sure I could not have written *Just Rest*, but I'm very glad I read it."

Robert Kurland
Writer for the Magis Center for Faith and Reason

"Sonja Corbitt does not just walk us through the deserts of life; she also helps illuminate those lonely journeys with the light of grace. But then, in a surprising twist, she also puts this life and light into the context of modern science. She helps us see God's presence in the desert and in the whole universe."

Stacy Trasancos
Author of *Particles of Faith*

"Embracing the story of the Exodus—but with a refreshing twist—Sonja Corbitt leads the reader through the strenuous desert journey with the children of Israel, showing how God dwelt with his people and cared for their every need, desiring for them to rest in his love. Using engaging personal stories, Corbitt invites us to pray the scriptures as she tenderly guides us through the deserts of our own lives, taking us through dryness and desolation to a springtime of spirituality. Like the dewfall, *Just Rest* gently nourishes the driest of souls. A must-read for anyone who could use a little spiritual spa time!"

Kelly M. Wahlquist
Founder of WINE: Women In the New Evangelization

"The human person has a habit of avoiding two things: suffering and rest. Sonja Corbitt does a beautiful job of not only giving us a new way of understanding these things but also bringing them together in order to find joy, fullness of life, and intimacy with Christ. This book is a must for anyone who has faced or is now finding themselves in the desert. Corbitt teaches us that the Exodus wasn't long ago but is here and now, a true gift for all of us."

Rachel Bulman
Contributor to Word on Fire Catholic Ministries
and cohost of *School of Humanity* podcast

"Having picked up *Just Rest* in a time of busyness and burnout, I was struck to the depths of my heart. With her usual biblical insight, Corbitt lays out why spiritual rest is more than just taking a break and invited me into the desert with her to find it. I left the book feeling renewed, refreshed, and ready to trust the God who leads his people out of bondage and into the Promised Land."

Shannon Wimp Schmidt
Cohost of the *Plaid Skirts and Basic Black* podcast

RECEIVING GOD'S RENEWING PRESENCE IN THE
DESERTS OF YOUR LIFE

JUST *Rest*

A STUDY OF THE EXODUS

Sonja Corbitt

AVE MARIA PRESS AVE Notre Dame, Indiana

Imprimatur: Very Rev. John J. H. Hammond, J.C.L.
    Vicar General, Diocese of Nashville
    Nashville, TN, 27 April 2021
Nihil Obstat: Rev. Andrew J. Bulso, S.T.L.
    Censor Librorum

Unless otherwise noted, all scripture quotations are from the *Revised Standard Version of the Bible—Second Catholic Edition* (Ignatius Edition), copyright © 2006 National Council of the Churches of Christ in the United States of America. Used by permission. All rights reserved.

LOVE: Listen, Observe, Verbalize, and Entrust® is the author's trademarked process for praying with scripture.

© 2021 by Sonja Corbitt

All rights reserved. No part of this book may be used or reproduced in any manner whatsoever, except in the case of reprints in the context of reviews, without written permission from Ave Maria Press®, Inc., P.O. Box 428, Notre Dame, IN 46556, 1-800-282-1865.

Founded in 1865, Ave Maria Press is a ministry of the United States Province of Holy Cross.

www.avemariapress.com

Paperback: ISBN-13 978-1-64680-086-5

E-book: ISBN-13 978-1-64680-087-2

Cover image © www.gettyimages.com

Cover and text design by Katherine Robinson.

Printed and bound in the United States of America.

Library of Congress Cataloging-in-Publication Data
Names: Corbitt, Sonja, author.
Title: Just rest : receiving God's renewing presence in the deserts of your life / Sonja Corbitt.
Description: Notre Dame, Indiana : Ave Maria Press, [2021] | Includes bibliographical references. | Summary: "In this book, the author expands on Hebrews 3-4 by describing how to rest in Jesus during periods of spiritual dryness"-- Provided by publisher.
Identifiers: LCCN 2021018077 (print) | LCCN 2021018078 (ebook) | ISBN 9781646800865 (paperback) | ISBN 9781646800872 (ebook)
Subjects: LCSH: Bible. Hebrews, III-IV--Criticism, interpretation, etc. | Rest--Biblical teaching. | Rest in the Bible.
Classification: LCC BS2775.6.R46 C67 2021 (print) | LCC BS2775.6.R46 (ebook) | DDC 227/.8706--dc23
LC record available at https://lccn.loc.gov/2021018077
LC ebook record available at https://lccn.loc.gov/2021018078

Contents

Therefore, as the Holy Spirit says,

> "Today, when you hear his voice,
> do not harden your hearts as in the rebellion,
> on the day of testing in the wilderness,
> where your fathers put me to the test
> and saw my works for forty years.
> Therefore I was provoked with that generation,
> and said, 'They always go astray in their hearts;
> they have not known my ways.'
> As I swore in my wrath,
> 'They shall never enter my rest.'"

Take care, brethren, lest there be in any of you an evil, unbelieving heart, leading you to fall away from the living God. But exhort one another every day, as long as it is called "today," that none of you may be hardened by the deceitfulness of sin. For we share in Christ, if only we hold our first confidence firm to the end, while it is said:

> "Today, when you hear his voice,
> do not harden your hearts as in the rebellion."

Who were they that heard and yet were rebellious? Was it not all those who left Egypt under the leadership of Moses? And with whom was he provoked forty years? Was it not with those who sinned, whose bodies fell in the wilderness? And to whom did he swear that they should never enter his rest, but to those who were disobedient? So we see that they were unable to enter because of unbelief.

Therefore, while the promise of entering his rest remains, let us fear lest any of you be judged to have failed to reach it. For good news came to us just as to them; but the message which they heard did not benefit them, because it did not meet with faith in the hearers. For we who have believed enter that rest, as he has said,

"As I swore in my wrath,
'They shall never enter my rest,'"

although his works were finished from the foundation of the world. For he has somewhere spoken of the seventh day in this way, "And God rested on the seventh day from all his works." And again in this place he said,

"They shall never enter my rest."

Since therefore it remains for some to enter it, and those who formerly received the good news failed to enter because of disobedience, again he sets a certain day, "Today," saying through David so long afterward, in the words already quoted,

"Today, when you hear his voice,
do not harden your hearts."

For if Joshua had given them rest, God would not speak later of another day. So then, there remains a sabbath rest for the people of God; for whoever enters God's rest also ceases from his labors as God did from his.

Let us therefore strive to enter that rest, that no one fall by the same sort of disobedience. For the word of God is living and active, sharper than any two-edged sword, piercing to the division of soul and spirit, of joints and marrow, and discerning the thoughts and intentions of the heart. And before him no creature is hidden, but all are open and laid bare to the eyes of him with whom we have to do.

INTRODUCTION

A Prayer for Dew

If you've prayed incessantly for lasting peace but believe God must not have meant it for you; if you're harassed by self-punishing, painful, or fearful thoughts or memories; if you've done numbers of Bible studies or read stacks of books on positive thinking and are still in pain, live in fear, or feel anxious or out of control; if the duties and demands of your life routinely leave you exhausted, sick, resentful, or frayed, you *need* the lessons of the Exodus.

Rest is not a luxury; it is a spiritual discipline. It is a gift.

Rest is a promise.

We dispose ourselves to receive the promise of rest through a disciplined desert process common to God's people from the beginning. The biblical Exodus story is a map through this desert process, showing us the disciplines that offer "dew"—God's renewing presence in the desert that leads us to the superabundance of rest.

As a living process, the spiritual desert is a paradoxical fertile emptiness, a place in which God himself, the Source of all that exists—including every potentiality and possibility—is eternally present in what appears to be a dry barrenness. The Exodus story teaches us that whatever we need in the deserts of our lives— physical provision, emotional relief, spiritual aid—is *especially* available in that place and time of emptiness and dryness. The children of Israel lacked water in their desert, yet the Water was with them all the time. Like them, we live in a type of "urgency fog" that prevents us from seeing that all we need is already there. But there is literally never a circumstance in which you don't have access to everything you need; in fact, it is inevitable that you will receive exactly what you need when you live from this fertile desert reality. How is this so?

God gives himself to us—to all creation—at every moment. Everything that is, exists and is held in being because God is actively observing it with love. As the sage says, "You love all things that exist . . . for you would not have made anything if you had hated it. How would anything have endured if you had not willed it?" (Ws 11:24). St. Catherine of Siena asserted, "Everything comes from love" (*CCC* 313).

In his first letter (epistle), John the Apostle tells us that he speaks from experience when he declares that "God is light and in him is no darkness at all" (1 Jn 1:5) and that "God is love, and he who abides in love abides in God, and God abides in him" (1 Jn 4:16). God himself, then—who is light and love—is the basis of the entire universe. This connectedness of processes is not merely spiritual; it's literal. God's light-love permeates all things, connects all things, and *sees* all things in an actual way that holds them in being. This is the understanding of the universe with which quantum physics and medical science have begun to wrestle.

We are learning that the basis of the universe cannot be reduced to smallest units or a predictable, mechanical structure, because the basis of the universe is *energy*, an infinite tissue of interconnected *living* processes inexplicably held together by "consciousness." The implications of the proven and provable realities of quantum mechanics shook both the scientists who first discovered them and those who have studied them since, plunging them into an ancient mystery that the scriptures, our Savior, and his apostles and mystics and doctors of prayer have assured us of for millennia: "In him we live and move and have our being" (Acts 17:28).

We are meant to rest in the fertility of our desert circumstances and live from this plenitude by practicing specific, predictable disciplines that God teaches his people in the desert. Following the children of Israel through the Exodus account in the scriptures taught me how to rest in desert paradoxes. Their struggles became a kind of "pillar of fire" by which the Holy Spirit led me through my own Great Desert. As such, this book is an invitation to consider the Israelites' desert experience—an intimately familiar biblical narrative for some—in a glorious new way. Whether you consider the Exodus a familiar, maybe even boring narrative, or a frightening "valley of tears," my intention is to pull you into the desert with new eyes and ears, a different awareness, in order to transform your mental, emotional, physical, and spiritual unrest into a promised land of inner Sabbath. This rich promised land is God's will for you, for me, for all of creation.

The Desert Awaits You

A dear friend of mine contacted me recently and asked me to pray for her. She had been called back for an ultrasound and biopsy for her left breast after a mammogram, as she had been having pain in the same breast that had been biopsied seven years earlier. She was afraid to draw a connection, but related that her own mother had had a biopsy in her left breast years before she had developed cancer, from which she died. After having seen the stark, horrifying realities up close and watching her mother suffer slowly through breast cancer to the end, my friend was suddenly, eerily faced with all the old memories and all the old grief along with the same possibility. She was terrified, with two weeks to wait and worry over her test results.

How are we supposed to rest through circumstances like this? Is it even possible? Can God really expect that of us? Why are we still tormented with fear when we pray fervently for rest? Over the next difficult days, I asked her some questions about her relationships and circumstances and shared the disciplines in this book with her. We explored her desert together. She had bad moments and bad days. But with my friend's exhortation and blessing, I can tell you that her answer to those questions is, "Yes! You can rest!"

For the first time since her mother died decades ago, she slogged through her cancer memories and fears and faced the possibility of her own cancer with what she called . . . "excitement." Yes, "excitement." Not excitement at the possibility of cancer, of course, but for all the healing insights and peace she was finally experiencing after decades of unrest. I will share her story of rest with you.

You and I were created to live every moment from the abundance of the Source who created the universe. We are invited to draw from that all-encompassing light and love that is always creating, always working, always at rest. And yet we often wander as the Israelites once did—through a dry, purposeless, worrisome existence in the desert wilderness, *unaware*, without ever reaching our promised land. Why is that? The desert was never meant to be a graveyard, but a place of transition—for them and for us.

What *must* we learn in the desert in order to reach the inner Sabbath? What is the reality our spiritual masters have always known, and that science is now confirming, but that we have not yet truly understood? "For good news came to us just as to them; but the message which they heard did not benefit them, because it did not meet with faith in the hearers" (Heb 4:2).

The Hebrews text at the front of this book, then, is not only a New Testament retelling of the Exodus, but also a primer on how to receive the infinite possibility of the desert, an instruction manual providing a much-needed blueprint of discipleship[1] for authentic *rest*. It is a guide to the desert's purpose, ways, and lessons, as well as the faith that can be found there—so that you emerge from the desert into the plenitude of the promised land, drawing continually from that infinite rest.

What do I mean?

It is in the desert that we experience who we most truly are. Without props. Without distractions. Without filters. The words for desert or wilderness—*midbara, arabah, eremos*—are referenced nearly three hundred times in the Bible and have always held deep religious meaning.

Because the geography of the Holy Land is such that the desert is located at a lower altitude than anything else in the surrounding area, it carried an ominous, even evil, stigma. My friend felt this ominous evil bearing down on her when her desert began with her abnormal mammogram. I too found my own Great Desert a terrifying, dangerous, barren place, where I clearly saw and felt the struggle with evil (Heb 3:12). It is quite an excruciating experience and can be painfully humbling to be reminded of one's insufficiency, neediness, and lack of virtue simultaneously in a personal desert season.

Yet in both the Old Testament and New, those who were willing to learn the lessons of the desert experienced the most expansive promised lands. They drew closest to God's heart and learned to rest in desert uncertainty, isolation, and deprivation, trusting that God would reveal himself intimately and speak to them in the still, small voice of eternity.

Abraham.

Moses.

Job.

Paul.

And of course, Jesus.

An Invitation

Why does God draw those he loves into these desert places, these painful seasons of life, these periods that people generally try to avoid? Because he wants us to *rest* in him. "They looked toward the wilderness, and behold, the glory of the LORD appeared" (Ex 16:10). We work so *hard* to avoid the seeming harshness and hardness of the desert, when all along it's the only place the mysterious rest of the Lord can ever be permanently possessed.

The desert is an invitation to experience the infinitely sustaining truth that every mental, emotional, physical, and spiritual thing you need is already provided to those with faith. "Therefore I tell you, whatever you ask in prayer, believe that you receive it, and you will" (Mk 11:24). How can we extract the awareness and truth of Jesus' literal statement? The desert knows.

The desert is a call to true rest, to awareness, to training, and to preparation for something else, often something that would be impossible to accomplish on our own. For the Hebrew people that Moses led out of Egypt, as we are reminded in Hebrews 3–4, it was to teach them important lessons about what it means to be free from bondage and oppression and to rest in God's love.

They spent forty years wandering, failing, and falling over and over, until another generation took the desert lessons to heart. We read in Hebrews 3,

> Therefore, as the Holy Spirit says,
> "Today, when you would hear his voice,
> do not harden your hearts as in the rebellion,
> on the day of testing in the wilderness,
> where your fathers put me to the test
> and saw my works for forty years." (Heb 3:7–9)

When the vultures circle, the water runs short, and resources dwindle, it becomes more and more difficult to stay faithful, to remain hopeful, to keep going, to continue looking for moisture and sustenance in the parched desert barrenness. Like the wandering Hebrews, we complain and stumble, hoard and bicker. And then . . . just as our restlessness seeks to overwhelm us and we are succumbing to despair, God sends it: the consolation in our desolation, the relief our soul so desperately craves, the renewed sense of his presence. The signal that our Sabbath is *here*, that the time to enter fully into that rest is always "now." The dew of heaven falls.

Dew of Heaven

Dew is a gentler, more subtle version of rain. Rain commands attention, as anyone ever caught in a downpour knows. We hear it in the relaxing cadence of a light shower and in the roar of a heavy thunderstorm. Dew, on the other hand, is silent. As one poet says, "When did the dew tell us that it was about to fall? Who ever heard the footsteps of the dew coming down upon the meadow grass? Who ever knew when it was descending? We see it when it has fallen; but who saw it come?"[2] While rain draws attention to itself, dew is silent and humble, falling gently in the dark, refreshing and nourishing all that parched and withered in the hot desert sun.

The Jews considered dew to be a greater blessing than rain.[3] Dew is dependable, while rain is less predictable. Dew generally falls at the darkest time of the night, in the pre-dawn hours while man and beast still slumber. Atmospheric water vapor condenses to form small droplets on the surface of the ground, an appearance that seems almost miraculous for its imperceptible formation.

Especially for those who grow their own food, dew is always a blessing, whereas rain can arrive too early or too late for crops or cause flooding and widespread damage. When the earth is baked and dry, a hard rain cannot penetrate it; the water runs off uselessly, often eroding the land along with it.

God withheld rain when the Chosen People fell into sin, in order to correct and draw them back to him. But dew was a symbol of grace, of God's constant goodness that does not depend on our actions or behavior, but proceeds from his unceasing, immutable, life-giving love for his children. "But your dead shall live, their corpses shall rise; awake and sing, you who lie in the dust. For your dew is a dew of light, and the land of shades gives birth" (Is 26:19, NAB).

Dew reminds us that in our darkest, driest, "deadest" times, God is moving. Even when we can't see or sense the hand of God, his dew is forming and moisturizing in unseen, quiet, and even miraculous ways. Like the dewfall, his mercies are new every morning. If you are parched—exhausted from work, worry, or wandering—a gentle refreshment awaits. The dew is coming. And with it, a miracle may fall as well.

The Jews understood the blessing of dewfall and even offered a special benediction, called the *Tfilat Tal* or "Prayer for Dew," each spring on the first day of Passover. Perhaps this prayer will offer you hope in anticipation of the rest awaiting you in the meaning of the dew: it is a refreshment, a gift, and a message from heaven—a source of blessing.[4]

> May dew fall upon the blessed land.
> Fill us with heaven's finest blessings.
> May a light come out of the darkness to draw Israel
> to you as a root finds water from dew.
> May you bless our food with dew.

May we enjoy plenty with nothing lacking.
Grant the wish of the people—that followed you
through the desert like sheep—with dew.
You are Adonai our God,
who causes the wind to blow and the dew to fall,
For blessing and not for curse.
Amen.
For life and not for death.
Amen.
For plenty and not for lack.
Amen.

About This Book

To help you process the material in a more personal, prayerful way, I have included features at the end of each chapter similar to those in my previous studies, including *Unleashed* and *Exalted*. The most important of these is a lectio divina exercise called LOVE the Word®. This four-step process—referred to as "the best modernization of lectio"[5]—allows you to engage a passage of scripture as follows:

L | Listen (Receive the Word.)

Pope Francis called Mary the "mother of listening" because she is available and attentive to God. I listen by opening my heart to receive the Word of God: Come, Holy Spirit. The Word that I hear and read today is a gift from him in answer to my prayers. I read the passage slowly. I savor every word, possibly emphasizing each in turn. I write down those words that linger in my mind.

O | Observe (Observe your relationships and circumstances.)

Remembering that I am in the presence of the Holy Spirit, I observe the events of my life with him in the same way that Mary pondered. How does this passage speak to the circumstances, relationships, habits, concerns, and problems of the past day? To what word, phrase, or idea is my attention drawn? How is the Holy Spirit guiding and encouraging me today through this passage?

V | Verbalize (Pray through your thoughts and emotions.)

As I linger with the Holy Spirit over all that has surfaced in my heart and mind through his Word, I verbalize what I think he is saying to me just as Mary did in the Magnificat. I talk to him freely about my thoughts and feelings. I write it all down as best as I understand it and ask him to confirm or deny what I believe he is saying. I will watch to see how he answers by surveying the events of this day and week.

E | Entrust (May it be done to me according to your word.)

Once I have decided on some action or inaction with his help and in his presence, I am often overwhelmed by the tenderness, patience, mercy, forgiveness, and generosity of God. I resist words now. As I remain silent and simply rest in him, I entrust him with every outcome: "Let it be done to me according to your word" (Lk 1:38).

The Word of God is a constant, daily source of dew in the deserts of life. Without it, I would never have known God's astounding provision and promise of rest and refreshment, and I certainly would never have been disposed enough to receive it. You will never truly rest until you establish this vital connection with God in the scriptures, because the desert heat never relents, the dangers never disappear, and the deprivations never cease. You must have dew to survive. Let us pray, now, that by our making use of the scripture exercises throughout this book, the Holy Spirit will teach us how to receive his unshakable rest every day.

ACKNOWLEDGMENT

I extend my deepest and warmest gratitude to Robert Kurland, PhD, formerly of Harvard and Carnegie Melon, who sits on the Board of Academic Fellows and writes for the Magis Center for Faith and Reason on physics and evidence for God. A fangirl of his, I could barely believe he said yes to reading and offering his considerable expertise to the book, and I am thrilled to have also made a friend in the process. Thank you, "Doc."

One

REST IN THE WANDERING—
GOD'S WAYS ARE DESERT WAYS

Entering the Desert

> Structures of sin . . . are rooted in personal sin, and thus always linked to the concrete acts of individuals who introduce these structures, consolidate them, and make them difficult to remove.
>
> —St. John Paul II, *Sollicitudo Rei Socialis*

I was an evangelical Christian and a young mother still wrangling my first toddler when the comfortable edifice of my spiritual idealism was utterly demolished by the political maneuverings of the very people who had nurtured my fledgling faith, people I had trusted implicitly. I remember surveying the one hundred–person denominational community one Sunday morning and thinking, *Church shouldn't be this way. Christians aren't supposed to be so deceitful.*

It began with a whisper campaign against the young pastor. Petty disagreements swirled up and around, fueled by Bible study small groups that nitpicked his sermons, his off-day overalls, and his wife's hat-wearing. Everyone took sides and justified them with perfectly suitable Bible verses. But their ugly gossip, full of poison, made them seem more like a pit of vipers than a flock of sheep.

I wasn't above reproach either. In fact, I remember very clearly when the Lord pointedly corrected me as I was airing my own complaints to him about the pastor. *Obedience is infallible*, he said to me.

In the end, it was a lesson I barely got to practice under that pastor, because he got fed up with us, took another position, and left; our church broke in half afterward. But that experience touched off a sandstorm that caused a great desert in my life, and it was in this desert that I learned the difficult but necessary life lessons—just like the Israelites in the story of the Exodus—that led me through the suffering and wandering (and dewfall) directly to my promised land.

But I'm getting a little ahead of myself. Let me start from the beginning.

Entering the Desert

My own desert wandering began in earnest on April 9, 2000. I know the day because my whole "desert chronicle" is in journals I kept over that decade. Like the Israelites, my desert was connected to a promise: during my daily study time in the scriptures, the Lord taught me about "the secret place of the Most High" (Ps 91:1 NKJV) and impressed upon me the desire to write a study on it. Also like the Israelites—who previously saw themselves as possessions of Egyptian taskmasters, but whose promise inspired them to consider themselves the Chosen Ones of the God of the universe, motivating them to face the desert ahead with greater courage—my promise gave me new identity, new purpose, and new boldness.

I wrote the study. Then I tried to get it published—and it was turned down by every Christian publisher in America. I kept working on it, sure that God had promised me a "land of victory." As the years passed, the failed attempts swirled around me like real-life sandstorms. I worried, *What if I'm wrong? What if I never really received a promise from God?*

With great excitement, I had followed a promise on an unfamiliar road straight into the desert, just like the Israelites.

In the Bible, the word *desert* means to lie waste. It's a desolate term, signifying "confusion, empty place, without form, nothing, vain, vanity, waste, wilderness."[1] What in your life is wasted, confused, empty?

By definition, the desert is barren and inhospitable, often the abode of wild animals and subject to extreme temperatures; it is an environment that most human beings step into reluctantly and fearfully. Only rarely do we enter deliberately.

But what if we were to stop dreading and resisting the desert and accept its necessity and inevitability? What if we welcomed the time we spent in those wastelands? What if we moved forward rather than looking back, confident that God is persistent in offering us such desert seasons because he wants us to submit to a kind of purifying purgatory, here and now, while we can still lean on the sacraments and prayers and support of others? What if leaning into those desert lessons is the key to the permanent— even eternal—transformation we need?

A Fruitful Wasteland

I'm not going to kid you—I did not enter the desert willingly or joyfully for my spiritual "extreme makeover." I spent three Lents with my hands up in surrender, wailing, "What more can I give up, Lord? You've already taken everything but my health and my family!" Indeed, I was sure I had entered into the spiritual equivalent of the Sinai Desert, a "great and terrible wilderness, with its fiery serpents and scorpions and thirsty ground where there was no water" (Dt 8:15).

But I now experience deprivations much more restfully, because the Israelites' desert taught me that God's ways are desert ways. I know that it is in these deserts that he moves and creates most powerfully. If I am experiencing desert deprivations or repetitions that resemble the Israelites, I know something wonderful is trying to happen. But before I could get comfortable enough with deprivations to cooperate with them, he had to teach me what rest really is. As we read in the third chapter of Hebrews,

Today, when you hear his voice,
do not harden your hearts as in the rebellion,
on the day of testing in the wilderness,
where your fathers put me to the test
and saw my works for forty years. . . .
As I swore in my wrath,
"They shall never enter my rest." (Heb 3:7–9, 11)

After years of captivity and forced labor, the Israelites needed to rediscover what it really meant to rest, too. It was for this very purpose that the Lord brought his people through the desert and left their experiences in the scriptures for us. God calls us to rest every day, and it is in their desert experiences that we learn where to find rest and draw from it—rest in thoughts, emotions, body, and in the depths of the soul.

Now, the desert the Israelites knew was not a big sand pile, like the Sahara. Most of the land in the Sinai and Palestinian deserts only needs water to make it fruitful, and this is why daily dewfall is so important in that area. The annual season of scant rain demonstrates their latent fertility, when the deserts grow carpets of herbs and flowers, almost overnight. Even today many desert dwellers are nomadic, since staying in one place too long will exhaust what few resources the desert can offer.

Israel first met the Lord in the desert, and thereafter the tradition was forever set that others might also be transformed there. In the desert they were challenged to establish an awareness of and connection to the Source of all that is—he who is light and life, who gives a rest Adam and Eve understood and maintained effortlessly in a garden paradise before the Fall. The Bible itself tells us that the lessons God taught the Israelites in the desert also serve as a warning and template for us in our own desert deprivations: "Now these things happened to them as a warning, but they were written down for our instruction. . . . Therefore let any one who thinks that he stands take heed lest he fall" (1 Cor 10:11–12).

The deserts we encounter are places of transition, places to pass through. When the struggle is finally over, the desert will be transformed by the dew of heaven:

The desert and the parched land will exult;
the steppe will rejoice and bloom.
They will bloom with abundant flowers,
and rejoice with joyful song. (Is 35:1–2, NAB)

And so it is for us as well: once our lessons have been learned, once love has triumphed over fear and the struggle has effectively been decided, our deserts will transform and blossom. That is the ancient knowledge of the desert I want to share with you through the scriptures, specifically through the Exodus story as it's found in Hebrews 3–4. Yet as we meander along this ancient road with the Chosen People, we have the unique benefit of modern science to help sustain us with its dew. We know something extraordinary by the scientific method that they could not measure then: this desert emptiness contains the same power that created and sustains the entire living, undulating universe.

Literally!

The Desert Is a Living Emptiness

When he was pope, St. John Paul II appreciated and supported collaboration between the sciences, theology, and philosophy. "The unity we perceive in creation on the basis of our faith in Jesus Christ as Lord of the universe . . . seems to be reflected and even reinforced in what contemporary science is revealing to us."[2] Indeed.

Contemporary physics shows us that the atom—the smallest unit of ordinary matter, invisible to the naked eye—is about 99.9 percent open space.[3] Proportionately, the space around the nucleus of an atom has been compared to a cathedral containing a single grain of rice. But the space in the atomic cathedral is not empty or dead. Rather, it appears alive with whirling activity, spinning around the grain-of-rice type nucleus. What we see and touch is a sort of condensation—a collapsing, if you will—of quantum states. At the subatomic level, the chair you are sitting in is a whirling, buzzing vortex of processes. Forests, wind, sound, color, oxygen, thoughts, emotions, your house, your car, your physical body, the stars, your dog, your ability to see, hear, smell, taste, touch—everything is interconnected by quantum processes.

What the Bible, Jesus, the apostles, and the Church have told us is true: all things are connected. Literally. Everything at its deepest level is a continuously vibrating process of energy that is intricately interconnected with everything else. Everything exists in a quantum state with particular energy. There is nothing that does *not* possess this energy. But the most astounding reality is that this base energy contains all possibilities at once, and in one interpretation of quantum mechanics, consciousness determines if or how the energy will collapse and become reality. This means that what seems to be dead, empty space in the desert also contains this energy, along with every possibility of what it could become.

Intention Matters

One model of the universe posits that we live in a world of non-physical space, within a quantum energy field that underlies the processes that make up the entire universe. It is a world that rests within a permeating reality, undulating and condensing in a way that creates what we perceive to be things.

This hidden reality exerts a continuous, complementary influence on the physical world, similar to the way your own consciousness affects your physical body. Your hand does not cause your finger to move; your brain does. This is exactly the idea St. Paul was conveying with his "Body of Christ" imagery in 1 Corinthians 12, in which each of us is an "organ" or member of the Body of Christ, who is our head. The parts operate together as their own distinct process, so that the whole is greater than the parts and is directed by the Holy Spirit, the mind of Christ.

Similarly, consciousness may be the means by which all visible reality exists and interacts. Physicists such as Raymond Chiao propose clearly that God is the ultimate conscious observer of the universe (think Big Bang); he and others hold that our own free choices (consciousness) also affect processes in time and space. Chiao's theological conclusion—that God is the omnipresent, omniscient, and omnipotent universal Observer, as presented in an essay[4] on quantum mechanics that I read with pounding heart and blurry eyes—will be the basis for our exhilarating exploration of the Israelites' and our own desert experiences. It reflects and reinforces what our faith and the scriptures have told us all along: we are cocreators with God of our own reality. Only focused attention, or consciousness, will cause energy to collapse into a thing. What will my focused attention draw forth in my desert? Will it be fear and deprivation, or will it be faith and provision?

There are many interpretations of the science, but there is widespread agreement on an interconnectedness to the universe that cannot be isolated into smallest units. The cosmos can be imagined, rather, as a complicated, organic network of energy that fuels relationships between individual processes and always includes the observer in an essential way. So we can never speak about the universe without speaking of ourselves, and every choice and action immediately and concretely impacts *the entire whole*.[5] Although we see and experience matter as solid, underneath it's whizzing around at these colossal velocities in a constant state of dynamic movement. It's only the forces between atoms that gives us the impression that anything is actually solid.

To put this quantum reality another way, anything and everything which exists in the entire cosmos, when broken down and analyzed in its purest and most basic form utilizing sophisticated scientific tools and instruments, is a combination of quantum states. The energies of these states, when observed, determine our perception of reality. As a result, our perception of reality, and that alone, determines what we experience as individuals in the physical world.

Think of your thoughts and emotions as focused spiritual energy that creates reality, either of rest or unrest. We are indeed cocreators with God. Everything visible emanates from the invisible in a constant interaction between the two.

God's ways are desert ways because the desert "emptiness" actually contains everything we need; we are meant to learn how to consciously cocreate with God all that we need in the desert, rather than allowing our own (often unconscious) negative energy to continue creating a defeating reality where we lack what we need and flail around in fear and unrest. Like the Israelites, we enter the desert to learn how to stop focusing mental and emotional energy on the emptiness. Instead, we focus our faith on the possibilities present in the spiritual light and love that animates and connects the universe. This faith focus is consciousness, and consciousness manifests all reality. Rest in thoughts and emotions is vital, because when we are not at rest interiorly, we manifest unrest exteriorly.

Back to the Desert: Repetitions and Deprivations

I readily and humbly admit that what I have presented here is a tremendous oversimplification of the science. However, even a simple description is necessary for this study, because it provides important context to the Israelites' wilderness journey and affects how we react in our own deserts—what we will or will not receive there, not just in moments of temporary physical deprivation, but also in emotional and spiritual wastelands as well. As we have said, God uses these desert encounters—in all their repetition and deprivation—to lead us to mental, emotional, physical, and spiritual rest.

St. John Paul II maintained that "both religion and science must preserve their autonomy and their distinctiveness. . . . Christianity possesses the source of its justification within itself and does not expect science to constitute its primary apologetic."[6] There is truth and beauty in science, but ultimately "we walk by faith, not by sight" (2 Cor 5:7). Most of us cannot and do not need to know all of the science. But knowing just a little opens up an entirely new world of rest and desert possibilities.

We can trust that God's wilderness ways have a unique and necessary purpose. We are truly, intimately connected beyond space, distance, nationality, or time to God himself and everything we need, to the children of Israel, and to all the saints that followed, experienced, and witness to desert truth (Heb 12:1). We must not abandon ourselves to despair in desert deprivations. We are surrounded by a great cloud of witnesses who know how to help us reach the inner Sabbath and how to receive dew in the desert.

The Call to Rest

The realities of my own perennial desert experiences—including the reasons for their existence—are something I ever so slowly and haltingly came to accept and understand through a personal time of intensive rest lovingly "forced" upon me by our heavenly Father.

After a second church split (more about that later), we left our home church. Whereas in the past I had been busy and vigorous in serving the church, I now found myself completely removed from serving at all. Lost, bewildered, and feeling a little punished, I questioned the Lord. After all, I had written a study in obedience to his promise. Why wasn't anything happening with that? Why was there absolutely no way to move forward?

What do you suppose happened next? I found myself in a daily study of the book of Hebrews.

A cursory read-through of Hebrews 3 and 4 hit me hard. I heard God clearly say that I must "be" rather than "do" for a while, that the downtime he had given me was a gift and that I must learn real rest in preparation to receive my promise. Even so, I struggled against the lack of action and "productivity." I objected, *But I'm not tired!*

As the days dragged on, I begrudgingly dug into Hebrews 3–4 and allowed the Israelites' example to instruct me. I finally began to understand that although I was ministerially inactive, I was not *at rest*. I was afraid—of uselessness, of wasting time, of loneliness, stillness, and boredom, and of missing my opportunity, because *What does it mean if I just stop trying to make my promise happen?* I thought often of what St. Josemaría Escrivá articulated, "To be idle is something foreign in a man who has apostolic spirit."[7] I felt untethered, floating in some terrifying, dark emptiness that led nowhere.

Why Does God Want Us to Rest?

God wants us to know rest, because rest is actually part of the definition of salvation. To have rest is to have God.

As I began to understand this, and to accept and practice God's view of rest, it changed forever my view of life, service, and ministry. Darkness in prayer, feelings of abandonment and detachment—none of that sways my intention now. Seasons of vigorous, even exhausting, activity and attacks on peace and rest are inevitable, but I am no longer tossed about by conflicts in focus and I recover as quickly as the unrest is identified.

I do not fret consistently for my husband or children's spiritual or physical safety. I know he loves them more than I do. I no longer worry about him providing for us; I know he will; and what he doesn't provide, I know we don't need. I do not fear failure, calamity, or scarcity; it will come, and he will work it into good (Rom 8:28).

I do not struggle with delays, lack of advancement, or "nothing happening" at work; I know his timing is strategic. I now view unexpected pauses in activity and work as God's great providence for me at that time in my life. In fact, I expect—and this is a biblical expectation, one that frees me to exert every possible effort during busy seasons—that he will provide those pauses for my rest. The isolation and silence he provides help me recover my stamina and prepare me to return to the active world of evangelization.

That first, terrible desert nurtured a deep, connected peace in me with both God and neighbor that continues to grow. Such mysterious peace is the dew of heaven—the grace of true, deep, biblical rest—and is the inner Sabbath promised to every single child of God.

What Is Rest?

In deprivation and suffering we experience our greatest challenges to rest and purpose. Why, then, does God convict us of unrest in our focal passage for this study, Hebrews 3:7–4:13 (included in the front of this book)? The passage warns of "evil unbelief," and the context is fear in desert seasons of deprivation: "Take care, brethren, lest there be in any of you an evil, unbelieving heart, leading you to fall away from the living God" (Heb 3:12).

I have practiced a daily quiet time in the scriptures for decades; I know when God is using a passage to speak directly to me, so I was stunned and disturbed by the implication when reading this passage that I was personally in danger of evil, of an "unbelieving heart," and of "falling away" from God. Those are dire words! I confess I was a little offended that God would so unfairly apply that verse to me.

When the Holy Spirit used these verses to convict me of unrest and teach me to understand rest from his perspective, I had served in church joyfully and faithfully for years—choir, leadership, mission trips, Bible study, Sunday school, VBS. I loved every minute; I prayed and studied my Bible every day; I wasn't resentful, I wasn't burned out, and I wasn't tired.

I made the mistake of judging the Lord's rest based on what most of us call physical rest. But God is not a man, and God's rest is not physical rest from weariness. We know, first, because God is spirit (Jn 4:24). Not "a spirit," as though he were one of many, but he is pure Spirit, pure existence, the I AM. Existing outside of time and space, there is nothing to see, hear, or sense of God unless he makes himself felt or sensed. Second, "The LORD is the everlasting God, the Creator of the ends of the earth. He does not faint or grow weary" (Is 40:28). The Lord does not rest because he is tired, and his rest is not physical, but spiritual, since he is Spirit.

I didn't feel physically tired, but I soon understood God wasn't talking simply about physical rest. He addresses "evil unbelief" in several other prominent areas that become clear in the Old Testament narrative. As such, the Hebrew passage did apply to me, and it applies to all of us, every day, but especially now in our unique moment of history where instant, constant communication and social media unrest are the background noise of our lives.

Fear Equals Unbelief

We will return to Hebrews 3:7–4:13 over and over as we unpack its riches together in the coming chapters, but for now, because it is the focal passage of this book and gives us concise instruction for dealing with all types of unrest, I ask you to turn to the front of this book and read it there in its entirety. Better yet, turn to Hebrews 3:7–4:13 in your own Bible. Read the passage slowly, without skipping, noting whatever arises in your mind and heart as you read.[8]

If I had to describe my impression of a first read-through of the passage that day, using only one word, I would say it felt *ominous.* As I studied, the unease multiplied in my heart, because I myself was wandering in a strange period of life and sensed I might somehow be in danger of forfeiting rest too. Especially since the context implies some deep significance aside from superficial stillness.

The text uses the wilderness wanderings of the children of Israel as a metaphor for unrest. Conversely, the promised land is presented as rest. Because "Today, when you hear his voice, do not harden your hearts," means right now, the Holy Spirit is speaking to you and me this very moment too, saying essentially, "Listen carefully to me now, and learn rest."

Rest is the absence of fear in every deprivation. In the story of the Exodus, God's people do not enter the promised land—they do not rest—because of an "evil, unbelieving heart" (Heb 3:12). Unbelief is evil because it leads away from God, as in the phrase "fall away." They do not believe (trust) because they are afraid. They are afraid because they are deprived in the desert—and might die that way. They live and die in fear outside the promised land *because they do not know his ways* (Heb 3:10–11).

Doesn't fear cause paralysis? Doesn't paralysis lead to stagnation? Doesn't stagnation lead to death?

I had only just entered my desert when I began studying this passage, with no idea of the suffering and adversity that awaited me. But it encouraged me to trust that my lack of activity had a distinct purpose. I needed to stop resisting it, because if I resisted the lessons offered, I might forfeit my promise just as the Israelites did.

We might put it this way: fear = unbelief = unrest. The paralysis of fear is why we must grow, strengthened by the dew of heaven, out of unrest and into mature love (see 1 John 4:18). Fear leads to forfeit. Faith frees from fear. Rest is in knowing his ways and cooperating with them.

The Way of Repetition

Isn't it interesting that God has *ways*? And that he expects us to know them? What are God's ways? Don't we seem to waste a lot of time and energy trying to accomplish balance and substantial change on our own, without seeking to understand God's ways? Learning his methods helps me discern where to look for his action, how to hear his instructions, how to yield, and how to work *with* him rather than against him.

The Holy Spirit has been at work teaching his people rest since the beginning of time and has always worked in particular ways. The Bible shows us that God follows certain methods in the way he speaks to and works in humanity generally and in you and me specifically. Isn't it comforting that he wants us to know his methods? He does!

"The LORD said, 'Shall I hide from Abraham what I am about to do . . . ? No, for I have chosen him, that he may charge his children and his household after him to keep the way of the LORD by doing righteousness and justice; so that the LORD may bring to Abraham what he has promised him'" (Gn 18:17–19).

Job declares, "I will teach you concerning the hand of God; what is with the Almighty I will not conceal" (27:11).

Amos concurs; "Surely the Lord GOD does nothing, without revealing his secret to his servants the prophets" (3:7).

Jesus told us, "No longer do I call you servants, for the servant does not know what his master is doing; but I have called you friends, for all that I have heard from my Father I have made known to you" (Jn 15:15).

When we grow fearful and confused, how often is it because we have no idea what God is doing? Why don't we know? Is he hiding it? Perhaps sometimes he must. But could it be we have not been listening to God in his Word to hear what he wants to do and *is* doing in our lives? God wants you to know his purposes and his methods, because when we know his ways, we are less likely to go astray in our hearts (Heb 3:10). Knowing God's ways helps us to cooperate with him and all he wants to provide for us, to receive from him, to rest in desert deprivation, and to offer that rest to those around us too. We become circles of rest.

The first method, or "way," in our text, is repetition. God repeats whatever he wants us to learn so we don't miss his working. I call these repeats "pop quizzes," because they are accompanied by surprising and often challenging applicable circumstances that invite us to practice what he is teaching. Over and over I hustled to "make something happen" regarding my promise, but I was thwarted pointedly and repeatedly. That's an example of a pop quiz. Pop quizzes are important because they show us where he is working and how to cooperate with him there. After realizing there was method to the madness, I submitted to inactivity, knowing it was somehow necessary. Repetition is one of God's ways.

Our text begins with a direct quote from Psalm 95, itself a reference to the original incidents in Exodus and Numbers that were reviewed by Moses in Deuteronomy. The section in Hebrews that contains this verse begins, "Therefore, as the Holy Spirit says . . . ," and then quotes part of Psalm 95. Essentially this sentence is an exclamation mark on the fact that God himself is saying this to us, *for a fourth time*, through the author of Hebrews. He said it first in the original accounts in Exodus and Numbers, reviewed it with the people in Deuteronomy just before they finally entered the promised land, repeated it a third time in Psalm 95, and then reiterated a partial quote of it here, in the letter to the Hebrews.

Remember when your mom used to say your first, middle, and last name and how you knew you had better heed whatever was said next? Whenever an idea is repeated this way in the scriptures, *especially* when the emphasis spans both Testaments,

God is saying, "Pay attention!" He is stressing the importance of something—about himself, his purposes, or his ways. I like to say, "Twice makes a pattern," but throughout the scriptures, the importance of these wilderness events to our spiritual lives is emphasized almost a dozen times! If I knew anything as I entered my desert, it was that I must heed the repeated warnings in the scriptures to heed the repeated warnings in the scriptures!

A Second Cancer Scare

The way of repetition in the Israelites' wanderings helped me to assist my friend who needed a biopsy to test for cancer in her left breast. When she told me that her mother had cancer in the same breast after having also had a biopsy seven years earlier, I recognized God's way of repetition immediately. Although a "fog of urgency" clouded the view for her, the circumstances seemed too eerily ironic to me to be anything other than an invitation to a different sort of plenitude in her cancer desert. Because my decades of ministry have involved significant experience with informal spiritual counseling, I sensed she was open to that suggestion. So I asked about her relationship with her mother before and during the cancer and about her mother's relationship with her grandmother. What an eye-opening revelation the answers to those questions became as the similarities in three generations of mother-daughter relationships came to light.

But the truth my friend came to rest in was that she had lived in suppressed, unacknowledged fear of cancer ever since her mother had first fallen sick. She thought of it often in the following decades with dread and anxiety, each year at her own mammogram, and especially now that she needed a biopsy just as her mother had needed. She was afraid to even say the word *cancer*, especially since she was confronted with the real possibility of having it herself. Was her fear of cancer making her sick? If not true physically, her fear of cancer had definitely stolen her rest for decades. She accepted God's invitation to learn a deeper rest; she learned how to transform her dark thoughts and emotions; she was excited to experience rest in this area for the first time in her life. She disposed herself to rest through the Exodus lessons, all by first recognizing the invitation in God's way of repetition.

The Way of the Word

As soon as I drew my friend's attention to God's way of repetition, I pointed out the lessons of the Exodus in the scriptures and the promise of rest there, because the second of God's methods, or ways, is that he communicates and transforms through his Word. Where does God share his purposes and ways with me so I can know what he is up to in my life? How do I avoid "evil unbelief" and receive refreshing dew in my busy, stressful routine? How do I steadily and clearly hear him speak to me personally about my diagnosis, scarcities, emotional eruptions, perfectionism, hurry, loneliness, self-medication, and busyness in ways that transform and bring rest? How can I truly rest in deprivation so that I can receive what I need in the desert?

Our text in Hebrews reminds us, "For the word of God is living and active, sharper than any two-edged sword, piercing to the division of soul and spirit, of joints and marrow, and discerning the thoughts and intentions of the heart" (4:12).

When reading large portions of scripture, it is often helpful to skim the chapter and paragraph headings to get the gist before reading a passage or book word for word. These headings depend on the translation you're using, of course, but in one translation the paragraph heading for the latter part of our text says, "The Word Discovers Our Condition." Therein lies our second principle for knowing God's ways: that the Word of God discerns and pinpoints the specific places and roots of unrest in our lives. This is how we, as St. Gregory says, "learn the heart of God from the word of God."[9] The heading's location at the end of the exhortation even intimates that the preceding passage has already somehow specified what has caused our unrest.

I realize that "The Word of God Discovers Our Condition" seems rather self-evident to those who read or study the Bible regularly. Perhaps you even rolled your eyes at such an elementary principle. However, due to the repetition spanning both

Testaments, and because every day is "Today" (Heb 3:7), perhaps we should not dismiss the repeated warnings so casually. Indeed, Moses in Deuteronomy specifically invites you to this refreshing dew: "May my teaching drop as the rain, my speech distil as the dew" (32:2).

God is stressing through repetition in his Word that the roots of unrest are revealed in the desert, through the anxiety, emotional eruptions, perfectionism, hurry, loneliness, and comfort-seeking provoked there. For instance, my friend had a second abnormal mammogram, and all of her latent cancer fears broke to the surface and threatened to overwhelm her, but that place of protracted unrest and fear (slavery) was where the Holy Spirit was working and inviting her cooperation.

Spiritual familiarity and routine, preconceptions, and lack of introspection conceal fear and its root. But "the word of God is living and active, sharper than any two-edged sword, piercing to the division of soul and spirit, of joints and marrow, and discerning the thoughts and intentions of the heart. And before him no creature is hidden, but all are open and laid bare to the eyes of him with whom we have to do" (Heb 4:12–13).

The Word of God is so incisive, there is no escape from its authority and no possibility of avoiding responsibility toward it. With subtlety and precision, it dissects the thinking spirit and emotional soul in a way that is personal and all-searching. No random string of thought, no stray emotion, no hidden intent is left untouched or unaddressed. The phrase "laid bare" before his eyes comes from Old Testament sacrificial practices, where an animal's neck was bent back and bared for the knife. The expression conveys that the Word of God acts on the neck, a biblical symbol of the will, which also explains why the Israelites were called stiff-necked people: they never learned the lessons of the desert because of stubbornness, not stupidity.

We must be careful to listen to his Word and allow it to judge us every day; first, because it influences our eternity: "But if we judged ourselves truly, we should not be judged [condemned]" (1 Cor 11:31). Second, rest is at stake: "For good news [the Gospel, or the Word] came to us just as to them; but the message which they heard did not benefit them, because it did not meet with faith in the hearers" (Heb 4:2). When we are attentive to his Word, we receive daily dew in the desert that can, if met with faith, lead us to rest. How does this work, practically?

In a general way, we learn what rest is by studying the principles laid out for us in the Hebrews passage, as we are doing in this book. Then day by day, as dew falls, either (1) we will encounter in the daily readings of the Church something that speaks to what is happening in our lives (what he is doing), and then experience a pop quiz about it, or (2) we will find ourselves living in a pop quiz and then find a daily measure of explanation or comfort in the readings.

Choices are made from free will; they can be redeemed, but never changed. Every relationship, connection, event, and circumstance of our lives is an opportunity to choose, and the desert pressure heightens both the stakes and the nature of the choice. When we don't discern the pop quiz for what it is, or do not learn its inherent lesson, we will be offered another one; I have noticed in my own life that similar circumstances repeated twice or more are a pattern. Have you noticed that the longer it takes to discern a lesson, the more difficult and painful your circumstances grow? Repetition is meant to attract our attention so we can cooperate with him in learning to rest and navigate ongoing difficulties in the Holy Spirit. See how God's ways of repetition and the scriptures work together? See how persistent God is in offering us opportunities to experience rest in his love? This is why Jesus said while in the desert, "Man shall not live by bread alone, but by every word that proceeds from the mouth of God" (Mt 4:4), a repetition of Deuteronomy 8:3!

As our Hebrews passage emphasizes, the scriptures are the path for progressing out of fear to rest in mature love, both generally in deeper study and specifically on a daily basis. The Holy Spirit speaks there often about the challenges specific to your individual desert. The Word of God accomplishes what it says (Is 55:11); when he speaks "Fear not" directly to your heart from his Word, your fear will flee. When you apply the promises in his Word, they accomplish what is promised.

The principle is that God's Word discerns the roots of our fear and unrest and helps us know how to proceed through desert pop quizzes. Rest is the ultimate reality, not anxiety and worry, even in work and deprivation. Especially in work and deprivation. We learn rest in the desert by knowing his ways through repetition and the scriptures.

Desert Ways

After stressing the importance of the exhortation (the message) through repetition, the Holy Spirit refers to the Israelites' forty-year wilderness wandering and specific fears they experienced there, distinct fears and unrest common to every human being, which we will explore throughout this book. The desert is an abandoned stretch of land, seemingly without protection, necessary sustenance, or vegetation—all of which are deprivations that play upon the imaginations of people.

But most of the universe appears empty like the desert, when all the while it's teeming with life and possibility! We can't see or touch this energy, but it's around us and in us, all over the place. There's a constant dynamic exchange of energy going on in a never-ending cycle. It's in the seeming emptiness, the space or void, where the underlying reality of all existence is, according to quantum physics. The desert is not empty or lifeless; it is full of possibility, and only needs the dew of observation to flourish into life.

The number forty is a symbolic, round number that indicates a time of gestation in preparation for new life; think a forty-week, full-term pregnancy. The children of Israel traveled for two years, spied out the promised land for forty days, and then wandered another thirty-eight years in futility after refusing to trust God by entering the land. Their forty years wandering in purposelessness corresponded directly with their forty days of surveillance in the promised land, a point we'll return to later.

Remember that wilderness is synonymous in the scriptures with desert and is a metaphor for the discipline of learning to dispose ourselves for rest—for the whole Church collectively and for each of us individually. The children of Israel show us that one of God's most predictable formation strategies is the paradox of his rest-producing desert ways. In fact, you can bet that multiple deprivations occurring simultaneously indicate you are in a season of intense spiritual formation. What do I mean?

Consider the pandemic, a time when we were all hit with multiple deprivations in several areas simultaneously: work and earning stopped, there were shortages at the grocery store, we feared sickness and death, financial worries multiplied, and worship gatherings were prohibited.

There were desert lessons to be learned. Sabbaths to be recovered.

In my experience, the desert is most difficult because of the removal of comforts and props—however holy they are—that I previously relied upon. He removes things, one by one or all at once, until it seems there is nothing left but a frightening space, void, emptiness. What is waiting to be born there?

Temporary deprivation is one of God's desert ways. It is meant to last only as long as it takes for us to learn how to find him and his provision in the emptiness, how to draw on his Being and Word in cooperation with him to receive rest: this is the lesson and purpose of the desert. Once that knowledge takes root in the deepest recesses of our souls, we rest in the "peace of God, which passes all understanding" (Phil 4:7). Because all our preservation instincts are provoked and pinging wildly, the Holy Spirit teaches rest most effectively in the lonely aridity of the desert. The deprivations are temporary, spiritual dew arrives daily through the Word, and it is God's promise that he is leading us to a land flowing with the milk and honey of rest.

From Fruitless to Flourishing

In the end, an entire generation of God's people declined his gift of the promised land by refusing to enter after their long but fruitless trial in the desert. God gave them up to his "wrath," a term that expresses not a sudden outburst that quickly subsides, but his abiding opposition to evil (see also Romans 1:18).

After repeatedly focusing on the temporary pressures and difficulties of deprivation through a lack of faith in God's provision, timing, and direction, the Israelites actually created a reality in which they were unwilling and unequipped to take the land. For forty days they observed the abundance of the promised land with doubt, and for forty years they wandered without it. Like Adam and Eve in the garden, only on a national scale, Israel's independent, disobedient spirit caused them to forfeit the plenitude God intended for them. But God was determined to bless his people. He sent a Messiah to teach us how to navigate the desert fruitfully. In navigating the desert fruitfully, he made it flourish for all of us.

Messianic redemption of the desert is a frequent theme in biblical prophecy, all of which is fulfilled by Christ. One such prophecy is found in Isaiah: "The wilderness and the dry land shall be glad, the desert shall rejoice and blossom; like the lily it shall blossom abundantly, and rejoice with joy and singing" (Is 35:1–2).

His messianic mission helps us to understand Jesus' own desert experience. As Israel's representative, Jesus experienced the same trials Israel had during the Exodus; what happened to Israel in the time of Moses happened to Jesus in the first century. Jesus, the new Moses, spent forty days in the desert, symbolically—but also actually—reliving and redeeming Israel's forty fruitless years in the wilderness. Through three temptations that mirrored Israel's trials in the desert, Jesus entered resolutely into the tension of their weaknesses and failings during their pilgrimage to the promised land.

Rather than resisting the lessons of the desert as had the ancient people of God, Jesus leaned into them. Why? Because he knew in every cell and atom of his being that provision was *already present* in the desert. In trusting precisely where Israel would not trust, Jesus revealed the lie of the empty desert and reversed its curse, both for the nation and for us all. Because Jesus was fruitful precisely where they were fruitless, the desert can be fruitful for you too.

In Jesus' battle with Satan in the wilderness, his response to the three temptations pre-enacts what he would ultimately do for Israel on the Cross: conquer sin and defeat the devil. This is the final battle Jesus fights and the ultimate liberation he offers. But he shows us the truth of the desert as well: everything we need exists wherever we are, even in the desert. Maybe even more so in the desert.

Jesus' first act as Messiah was to claim a series of desert victories over the enemy that had never been won before and that set the tone for the rest of his public ministry. All of his subsequent actions—healing the sick, forgiving sins, exorcising demons, and raising people from the dead—*depended* on of Jesus' initial triumph over the devil in the desert. What extraordinary implications this has for anyone who finds himself in the desert! Through grace, *what might I be capable of* if I allow God to teach me the lessons of the desert?

Jesus went from town to town carrying out his victory in the lives of the people he met. In touching the lives of the sick, crippled, blind, sinners, and demoniacs, Jesus freed them from the power and effects of unbelief, so that they could experience God's love and provision in their own lives. All this, of course, points forward to Jesus' work on the Cross, where he definitively conquered the enemy and won rest for all humanity (cf. Jn 12:31).

Jesus redeems the wasted places for all of us, so that what is meant by the enemy to discourage and defeat us becomes a place of growth, blessing, refreshment, and plenitude. His desert experience teaches us that effective service occurs out of who we are, not what we know, and that we become more of who *are* (who we were created to be minus sin) when we engage in the desert battle that the enemy brings against our common fears.

Welcome the Dew

You may be saying "No thanks" to the Bible's uncompromising invitation to learn a deeper rest in the desert. True, we have free will and can certainly resist what the Holy Spirit offers.

But if we don't do the learning and detachment work now, we will do it in purgatory, where the *ultimate* removal of every possible comfort and prop in the purifying fire of God's love is a far more difficult, unrelenting experience. "Today, when you hear his voice, do not harden your hearts." We can yield to the desert with new knowledge and confidence now, knowing that he always sends the dew to refresh and renew us, and that the inner Sabbath we receive ourselves also reverberates throughout the whole, bringing new measures of peace to a dark world through our invisible connectedness in God.

As I withered in my desert, one precious bit of dew sustained me every time I drew upon it. I still meditate on this frequently. I was lonely and so tired. I cried, "Where *are* you?" I was praying at the time (writhing really), frustrated that my prayers seemed to float out into empty space somewhere, unanswered. He asked, "What do you see?"

I had my eyes closed. I said, "Nothing!" and snorted, since it was black behind my eyelids. A shiver shot through me when he said, "You see everything." Everything we need already exists in him. As St. Teresa of Avila said, whoever has God lacks nothing; God alone suffices.[10]

Remember that pop quizzes are surprise invitations to put into practice what he is teaching? I imagine you have experience with the desert. I hope you will consider the possibility that this book is meant as dewfall to aid you in understanding and navigating your difficulties and fears in that regard—as he says, "May my teaching drop as the rain, my speech distil as the dew" (Dt 32:2). Why waste the graces offered in the opportunity to turn deprivation into plenitude, both for ourselves and those we love and serve? Why let the inevitability of desert experience be a merely painful time rather than a promise of gestation and giving birth to something new? Why not lift the tender flower of your face and welcome the dew?

The Promised Land

The Israelites' journey through desert unrest led to the promised land. Our text uses the term "sabbath" (Heb 4:9), meaning "rest," and expresses the term, ultimately, in an eschatological sense: there remains an eternal "Sabbath," or promised land, a promise of final rest at the end of life and the end of time. But in between, "there remains a promise of rest" in every deprivation, here and now, for each of us. I call it the inner Sabbath.

When the Israelites needed to learn rest, God led them into the desert. Just like our scriptural ancestors, the Holy Spirit began revealing the truth about my unrest through an intense desert experience (what I referred to earlier as a **pop quiz**). I was "benched" from ministry and spent a few years in the wilderness, wandering around, wailing and gnashing my teeth. My relationships were painful; my finances withered; my prospects disappeared; my promise shriveled; my prayer was dry (notice the pattern or **repetition** here). At first, I resisted inactivity and fought against feeling punished or disobedient for neglecting to use my gifts; I hustled to "make something happen"; I did not want to be guilty of not doing my part. But every attempt was thwarted, and my frustration grew, until, abruptly, the Holy Spirit revealed through his Word that he was teaching and calling me to rest (**dew** of refreshment arrived through the Word).

Startled to discover I was resisting him, I leaned in. I welcomed (albeit reticently) each difficulty and **deprivation**, realizing it would teach me something valuable if I could endure it. I received a little dew with each struggle that helped me trust, **rest**, and obey. I had absolutely no idea then that the lessons I would learn in that long, lonely, dry, barren interval would lead me to the Catholic Church, provide healthy ministry principles, and prepare me for the thrill of labor in my own **promised land**: balancing an intense prayer life, study, and daily worship; marriage; homeschooling; housework; child-rearing; hobbies I love;

book launches, writing, and ministry admin; television and radio shows; leading pilgrimages; hosting retreats; personal consultations; and weekly travel. I know I would never be able to do it well or fruitfully without remaining faithful to what the Holy Spirit taught me about rest during that desert. But looking back, I am stunned and deeply grateful that he was so patiently determined that I should learn!

Jesus did not need to learn to rest in deprivation; Jesus *is* rest in deprivation. But he did submit to God's purpose for the desert and used it to redeem our own, in the process setting healthy principles that would guide his forthcoming activity, his ministry of redemption. Jesus knows the secrets of the desert and teaches them to us. Besides peace and rest, what might your desert be preparing you for?

You may be hoping for a promotion or increase at work. Likely you pray for more balance in marriage, children, home, and church. Maybe you're waiting for your "person" or struggling through a difficult relationship. Possibly you long for the time when you can do more financially than barely get by. You might need rest from emotional and behavioral eruptions. Perhaps you anticipate a role in ministry. Could be you're just bone weary of it all.

The dew is falling.

True sabbath, true rest, is tapping into that vast creative unity throughout the cosmos that is the light and presence of God. "Your dew is a dew of light" (Is 26:19). The Amplified Bible, Classic Edition, says it this way: "Your dead shall live [O Lord]; the bodies of our dead [saints] shall rise. You who dwell in the dust, awake and sing for joy! For Your dew [O Lord] is a dew of [sparkling] light [heavenly, supernatural dew]; and the earth shall cast forth the dead [to life again; for on the land of the shades of the dead You will let Your dew fall]."

No matter what form our promised land takes in life, until we arrive at the final promised land in God's presence, every one of us must use the gift of his rigorous desert season to learn proper rest in order to be a good steward of his time and territory when he arrives. If the lessons of the desert do not penetrate, we will not enter at all, or our stay there will not endure; we will not survive the rigors of battle; we will burn out and grow resentful, succumb to discouragement, fall away, and may even turn away from the faith altogether. God's promise for your life, both in heaven and on earth, is rest; it simply awaits your undivided attention.

Let's Review

Let's review God's ways in leading us to rest.

- God's Word promises me rest.
- God's ways are desert ways. He calls me to rest every day. "Today, when you hear his voice . . ."
- Learning to rest requires desert seasons. The desert teaches us rest in thought, emotion, body, and soul.
- The path to rest is through God's Word. The scriptures identify areas of unrest in my life and the root of fear or disobedience beneath.
- God works through repetition. He allows "pop quizzes" and circumstances of deprivation that help me to apply what he is teaching.
- The Holy Spirit works most deeply in desert times.
- God always sends dew to refresh me in the desert; there is always a blessing awaiting me. I should ask and look for it.

An Invitation

Throughout this chapter, we considered that rest is not simply a lack of activity, but freedom from anxiety and fear in every deprivation. The Holy Spirit leads us to rest, "today," by teaching us God's desert ways.

Next we will go to the desert with the Israelites and look at several infamous incidents in their history specifically referenced in our focal passage, because "these things happened to them as a warning, but they were written down for our instruction, upon whom the end of the ages has come" (1 Cor 10:11). We'll probe how to avoid repeating their mistakes by learning to rest in God's provision and timing.

Then we'll explore how negative emotions and emotional eruptions trap us in a continual cycle of unrest, and discover how to prevent inevitable dark emotions from becoming unrest. We'll look at how perfectionism is a sign of deep fear and examine its root and fruit.

After that, we'll explore Sunday and other "times of refreshing" as divine prevention for impatience, resentment, and burnout. Finally, we'll discover that the lessons we learn in the wilderness are what sustain and help us thrive in the bustling activity of the promised land. We learn in a way that sustains us forever that there is always dew in the desert.

Benediction—LOVE the Word

As we finish this chapter, perhaps you have discerned a potential pattern in your weariness and are tired of wandering. Refreshment is waiting.

The next steps in your journey from unrest to the promised land will entail your listening closely to the promptings of your own heart and taking notice of what God is trying to say to you. You may want to flip back to the first page and read the chapter again, this time noticing the places that caused a strong reaction of some kind—perhaps longing, perhaps anxiety, perhaps a flash of insight.

Take a moment to invite the Lord to show you the patterns of unrest in your life. Invite him to reveal to you where he is at work, and trust that he will speak gently, steadily, and daily through the scriptures, like the dew. Even if he leads us to experience painful, lonely desert times, we can have faith that when we cooperate with him, they will also flourish with fruit.

What was the most significant sentence, idea, or paragraph you read in this chapter? If you are amenable to making marks in your books, I hope you will mark sentences or sections that stand out for you in some way. I often draw light bulbs or exclamation marks next to important sentences or ideas when I am reading.

Right now God is working all around me and my life. I long to experience the freedom of having all I need, but often fail to realize that plenitude is already available to me day after day, because I simply have not learned how to recognize his ways. If anything particularly struck you in this chapter, could it be the voice of God, already acting and moving in your heart and life?

Attempt to discern the pattern: can I use the principles from this chapter (see the Let's Review section) to identify an area, pattern, or circumstance in which God is already at work in my unrest?

L | Listen (Receive the Word.)

As with so many concepts we read about in the Bible, the first time it is mentioned is key in understanding its significance. In Genesis 27:28, Isaac blesses Jacob with these words: "May God give you of the dew of heaven, and of the fatness of the earth, and plenty of grain and wine."

As you repeat the following verse in his presence, try personalizing it and emphasizing each word or phrase in turn. Ask him to speak to your heart very clearly through this verse. You might try it like this:

> "*Lord*, give me of the dew of heaven."
> "Lord, *give* me of the dew of heaven."
> "Lord, give *me* of the dew of heaven."
> "Lord, give me *of* the dew of heaven."
> "Lord, give me of *the* dew of heaven."

Continue emphasizing each word or phrase in turn until you have focused on them all.

O | Observe (Observe your relationships and circumstances.)

What has God said to you through this chapter, and what does this verse say to you about unrest and fear in your relationships and the events in your life right now?

V | Verbalize (Pray through your thoughts and emotions.)

Lord, I am unrestful here . . .
   Lord, I need . . .
   But I am most afraid of . . .

E | Entrust (May it be done to me according to your word.)

Lord, I receive. Lord, I believe. Help my unbelief. Amen.

As one who served in church faithfully, followed God relentlessly, and lived in prosperity and comfort, I assumed my soul was in good shape and I was living as close to God as possible. Then disaster hit, fear took hold, and the wailing and gnashing of teeth began. The desert provoked scathing unrest, revealing destructive, hidden attachments and faults. God began explaining what he was attempting to teach through Hebrews 3–4.

The answers to the roots of your unrest also lie in the desert. Let us go together, then, to Marah, Massah, and Meribah.

Two

THOUGHTS AT REST

Testing in the Desert

O that today you would listen to his voice!
Harden not your hearts, as at Mer'ibah,
as on the day at Massah in the wilderness,
when your fathers tested me,
and put me to the proof, though they had seen
my work.

—Psalm 95:7–9

Although I had always dreamed of writing books, I had no idea why God had promised me that I would share with others the things he was teaching me through the scriptures. My education didn't fit the Bible-study teacher mold, I was in no position to afford or carve out the time to remedy my educational shortfalls, and every corner of the evangelical landscape I was part of was already crowded with aspiring wannabe preacher types, even in the women's arena.

But somehow, that I had "heard" it from God lent a gravitas and certainty to the endeavor that made it intolerable for me to ignore or abdicate. I knew nothing is impossible for him, and I believed with every fiber of my being that he was going to bless my effort and trust. So I went all in, investing all my heart, soul, mind, and strength in working to make my wonderful promise come to life.

For a long time, I was unsuccessful. With every rising obstacle and rejection letter, I was forced to peer behind a veil of fear and doubt and decide anew whether I was wasting my time in pursuing God's promise. Had I really heard from God, or was it all wishful thinking? Should it really be this hard if it was something I was *supposed* to do? With each rejection, my heart turned more and more inward as I floundered to make that promise come true.

As I struggled, I thought about the troubled relationship I'd had with my own father and wondered if God had been stringing me along like my father had done throughout my formative years: holding the proverbial carrot in my face to keep me jumping through hoop after hoop to prove my worth. Was failure after failure punishment for some hidden sin? Was I too "bad" or unworthy for such a wonderful gift? I grew more and more spiritually tired, increasingly disgusted with God and myself at how arduous every little step seemed to be and how little progress I seemed to be making.

Over that decade, as I continued to study and apply this Hebrews text, I began to see that my own spiritual journey had fascinating parallels with that of the Israelites in the desert: I wasn't *in* the desert—I *was* a desert, almost carrying it with me, wandering around with seemingly no direction and no forward movement. My focus remained on the promise, but God's focus was (apparently!) elsewhere.

As I grew angrier and increasingly suspicious that I had been duped, something deep within me just. would. not. give. up. And I felt stupid for persevering. Stupid that I had trusted some silly promise I had likely invented, and that God was probably laughing at my futile attempts to reach it. My greatest fear, rejection, was being realized, I felt, and it terrified me.

Can you relate to these feelings of worthlessness and disillusionment? Keep reading, beloved. I want to save you the time wasted wallowing in that gut-wrenching suspicion. And I also need to tell you *that your greatest fears will be likely confronted in the desert.* It's inevitable. And it's important. The most fruitful way forward, one I wish I had known sooner, is to confront that reality head-on. Let's turn to the Israelites to find out why.

Therefore as the Holy Spirit Says . . .

The Holy Spirit, the author of scripture, cautions us at the outset of the Exodus narrative in Hebrews through the warning stanzas of Psalm 95: "Today, when you hear his voice, do not harden your hearts as in the rebellion, *on the day of testing in the wilderness, where your fathers put me to the test* and saw my works for forty years" (Heb 3:7–9, emphasis added).

Psalm 95 is just one of many biblical summaries of the desert wanderings of the people of Israel. The words *rebellion* and *testing* refer to specific locations (Meribah and Massah[1]) where the people complained and rebelled. Later in the scriptures, the terms became a kind of spiritual shorthand for the entire quarrelsome, forty-year wilderness journey in which the people repeatedly tested God with suspicious accusations and emotional eruptions whenever they were confronted with their own needs. In fact, the *Catholic Commentary on Holy Scripture* says the writer of Hebrews "heightens the picture of the Hebrew rebellion by making the forty years a constant repetition of Meribah and Massah."[2]

St. Paul does something similar in 1 Corinthians 10, conflating the whole forty years into a single passage, a litany of the Israelites' willful ignorance: their indulgence in immorality and idolatry, their ongoing failures in observing God's direction. The Bible is full of summaries of how, every day, they forgot the miracles of yesterday.

In the numerous desert difficulties experienced by the Israelites, we can see *principles* that help us to better understand our own desert experiences—principles in thought, emotion, body, and soul—meant to dispose us for rest. This chapter examines Marah, Meribah, and Massah as particular episodes in the entire forty-year wilderness wanderings in order to draw out the primary obstacles to be mastered for making it through the desert fruitfully.

After resting in the necessity and inevitability of desert-wandering seasons and anticipating God's ways of engaging us there, the first obstacle we confront is our own thoughts. The remainder of this chapter addresses our thoughts as obstacles to rest, because the Israelites' unrestful thoughts determined their unrestful reality.

A Matter of Perception

The Lord had spoken to me. I had a promise.

Or did I?

The sea had split. The enemy was drowned. The Israelites were free.

Or were they?

Looking back upon my earliest memories, I can see clearly that my greatest fear was rejection. My father left me with a deep wound; he said there was something inherently wrong with me, and I believed him. For a long time, I had no idea that fearful wound was there, only that I had major anger issues.

When God began to heal me through the scriptures, I became gradually aware of the wound and its root and began to look to God as my true Father. Because of those feelings of unworthiness, I found myself in a never-ending cycle of working to please this Father as well, fearful that he would withdraw the reward of my promise from me just as my earthly father had repeatedly done. Like that of the Israelites, my relationship with God grew out of a bondage to deeply rooted fear.

God wanted to expose this wound and heal it at its root, and in order to do this he led me through my own desert wandering. I thought my promised land was being published; he knew my promised land was love beyond all praising. The promise of becoming a published author was simply my "way of the desert" to expose and heal the deeper need. While my focus was on the promise, his focus was on my freedom.

The Israelites' four hundred years of slavery in Egypt had also burrowed an invisible spiritual wound in their collective psyche. As God drew them into the wilderness toward healing, they were full of their own suspicions: was God simply a new Master intending to enslave them again? Would he really give them such wondrous prosperity and opportunity, or was he leading them to further dependency and servitude? I believe this was their greatest fear, and that the desert was meant to expose and heal that woundedness and mistrust. The Israelites' own words, repeated multiple times in the narrative, bear this out.

The details are related in Exodus and Numbers. The newly liberated nation was on the way to the promised land, but a scorching wilderness with its unending landscape of uncertainties lay between. There were no taskmasters to respond to their cries—only an invisible God through an inadequate leader, Moses.

Thirst for Freedom

In his infinite wisdom, the Lord began their basic lessons in desert fruitfulness by exposing their inability to meet their own most elementary needs. Their final week among the Egyptians—which included the unrelenting barrage of plagues—had been intense and dangerous, and their plight did not improve as they fled their captors toward the Red Sea. Then suddenly, miraculously, it was over.

After three days of travel in which the people faced the inherent desert dilemma of finding water for their families and cattle, they set up camp near a group of shallow wells they found at a place known as "Marah." Their stress and thirst catapulted to panic, however, when they discovered that although it was plentiful, "they could not drink the water of Marah because it was bitter" (Ex 15:23).

Right out of Egypt, they had nothing to drink! How could that be, when the last clear memory they had of their land of bondage was . . . a deluge of water at the Red Sea? How could God be rescuing them and leading them toward the promised land of plenty when they didn't even have this most basic necessity?

One eighteenth-century Jewish teacher, the Maggid of Mezeritch, observed that when *Marah* is translated literally, the Hebrew words are better translated "because *they* were bitter"[3] rather than "because *it* was bitter." According to this view, the undrinkable water at Marah was a result of the bitter attitude the people had brought with them; the bitterness in their hearts determined their experience of the water itself.

There is also an allusion to the people's underlying need and God's heart for them in the promise he offered at Marah, which intimates the purpose of their desert thirst: "I am the LORD, your healer" (Ex 15:26). Clearly something deeper than physical thirst is going on here.

The Jewish historian Josephus relates that the people were terrified at Marah. They "contended" with, or "murmured against," Moses for water (Ex 15:24). Moses prayed for drinkable water at Marah, and, believing, he lowered a tree down into the shallow wells. The Church Fathers see this tree as a foreshadowing of the Cross. The Israelite men were instructed to dig, draw, and agitate the water until it was clear, "that when the greatest part was drawn up, the remainder would be fit to drink."[4] They were able to drink, but only after great difficulty.

Notice that God heals the people's bitterness with their participation.

He doesn't permanently and magically "poof" it away, because they don't realize it's the real problem yet. But he is demonstrating a desire and ability to transform bitterness.

Perhaps the unexpected bitterness and labor involved at Marah is why the whole congregation contended again with Moses a month later at Meribah and Massah. *Contended* is a strong word often used to describe judicial arguments. The Israelites' legitimate concern spilled over in accusations of murderous intent, accusations God received against himself. Their provisions, which had lasted a month, were gone. They were angry enough to accuse God of slowly killing them in the desert.

Have you ever accused God, either aloud or secretly? I have, too many times to count.

The Israelites had witnessed the ten plagues, been released by Pharaoh with treasure and spoils, watched the miraculous parting of the Red Sea and crossed its dry seabed to safety, celebrated the destruction of their Egyptian enemies, and quaffed sweet water, first at Marah and later at the twelve springs of sweet water God provided as welcome relief from the barrenness of the wastelands (Ex 15:27). After repeated miracles, surely they could see that providing sufficient water for them now would be a small thing?

Yet they clearly had not learned the lesson, for the people began to quarrel with Moses again at Meribah (Ex 17:2). God responded by providing a geyser, plenty of water, from a most unexpected place. He took care that it came to them without any labor or difficulty, gushing out of a rock. It was a new pop quiz—different place and time, different circumstances, but similar to the last experience (Ex 17:1–7).

What should have been a precious discovery of God's tenderness and ability and *desire* to provide for them became notoriously bitter, as the place of the ordeal received the names "Massah," which means "place of testing" (or "proving"), and "Meribah," "place of quarreling." There, the people's deep lack of trust sprayed forth in ugly words as freely as the water from the rock, "for out of the abundance of the heart [the] mouth speaks" (Lk 6:45).

What are we to make of this?

Meeting the needs of such a large number of people and flocks on a journey such as this one must have been an immense challenge; there would have been no sin in asking for water. There is certainly no sin in *needing* water.

What is it about neediness that makes us leap to judgment when we see it in others or ourselves? Why are we embarrassed and panicked by neediness? Why do we get angry over and cover it and pretend and lie about needing what we need? Fear. Fear of what?

Well, that's what the desert is meant to reveal.

God's people were free from the Egyptians, but they were enslaved to fear, and God in his infinite tenderness longed to heal their terrible, bitter memories and free them from that even greater enemy. Do bitter memories enslave you? The Lord whispers dewdrops over you: "I am the LORD, your healer."

For every complaint, he provided what they needed. But by fixing their attention solely on present misfortunes, and continually complaining about them, they kept the deficits in the forefront of their minds. And because they failed to remember the litany of deliverances they had already experienced, they were hindered from anticipating what spectacular thing God might do next.

Had they been even nominally thankful, God's provision from the rock would have been a blessing. Sadly, because of their chronic discontent, the place that should have been associated with blessing remained marked with their bitterness. All because Moses's generation refused to trust God to provide for their needs in the desert. But Jesus shows us the better way.

Resisting Temptations in the Mind

In his own desert experience, Jesus was also challenged by Satan to test God by throwing himself off the pinnacle of the Temple, to see if the angels would miraculously save him (see Matthew 4:5–7). Unlike the Israelites, Jesus had absolute confidence in *who he is in the Father* and knew there was no need to stoop to proving himself or forcing God to prove himself. He viewed this temptation as parallel to Israel's water trial in the desert, responding to the devil by quoting part of Deuteronomy 6:16: "You shall not put the LORD your God to the test, *as you tested him at Massah*." Unlike the restless, angst-ridden throng at Massah, Jesus rested in his relationship with God.

In this gospel narrative, Jesus redeems the prior failure of God's Chosen People to trust God for what they needed—and he shows us, in his words and example, how we are to respond when we are tempted to doubt God's provision or timing.

As God's child, you do not need to force or manipulate him into proving his love; he *will* prove his love to you in spectacular ways as you engage in relationship with him. We must never demand a miracle or make our trust in God conditional upon a certain outcome. Such a demand is itself a lack of trust: this would be "tempting" God, or "putting him to the test." Instead, we must resist the natural tendency to fear, explore every option available, and wait as long as it takes for him to provide.

In your desert thirst for community, for understanding, for love, for provision, for protection, perhaps you can lean into "bitter." Name the place of your desert struggle "Bitter." Internalize and utilize the power of Bitter, the extraordinary force created by the voids in your life. Rather than complaining, "I have no water!" or "The water is bitter!" we can pray, "Where is the water?" or "Lead me to water," grateful for what is already freely available.

What should the Israelites have learned—what are we to learn—from each of these episodes, pop quiz after pop quiz on provision? To ask for what we need and wait for God to provide it. It's that simple. No drama, no complaining, no hand-wringing or accusations. You might get water . . . from a *rock*.

Angels' Food

Barely a month after their departure from Egypt, the Israelites' growling bellies clamored for attention. Their flatbread had run out, and they needed a reliable food source. But God's people did not know his strange desert ways; they were unaware their need was an invitation to intimacy with God.

It was time for another pop quiz for the Israelites. Again they were challenged on the issue of basic provision, this time for food. They were restless and scared, and they gave voice to their fear. "Would that we had died by the hand of the LORD in the land of Egypt, when we sat by the fleshpots and ate bread to the full," they complained to Moses, "for you have brought us out into this wilderness to kill this whole assembly with hunger" (Ex 16:3).

Again, rather than simply asking and trusting God for what they needed, they doubted and accused. This is the second time they accused God of wanting to murder them, made all the more outrageous because of all they had seen to the contrary. How quickly their jubilant praise at the Red Sea turned to indictment when thirsty and hungry under something of a forced fast. Were they in danger of remaining so with no food in sight, or was the desert "emptiness" alive with possibilities for food? "As I gave you the green plants, I give you everything" (Gn 9:3).

I don't know about you, but I can truly understand why they might have acted this way. Nothing draws out my inner witch like hunger. I am sure Snickers had me in mind when they said, "You're not you when you're hungry." Most of us have never worried where our next meal will come from, but fear of actual starvation had the Israelites looking back on the hardness of their oppression in slavery and seeing only the delights of a full stomach. Maybe you can relate: have you ever considered eliminating a destructive habit or relationship that enslaved you, peered into an unknown future without it, and justified keeping it, destruction and all?

The Lord seemed to understand this as well, and responded to the accusation with a miraculous and equally mysterious celestial gift. A special, nutrient-complete "bread" appeared with the dew on the desert floor, ready to eat—the first Frosted Flakes.

The people accepted it with piqued curiosity (Ex 16). They named it manna, meaning, "What is it?" Enough manna fell daily for each person, with a double portion appearing the day before the Sabbath, on which no manna fell.

Because it fell miraculously from "heaven" with the dew, it became known as angels' food (Ps 78:25). Manna had to be collected before sunrise, for despite its hard graininess, it melted in the sun with the dew. The quantity made exactly one portion for every person, whether one collected a lot or a little. Fine white and frosty flakes, manna was sweet as honey and "ministering to the desire of the one who took it, was changed to suit every one's liking" (Ws 16:21). Ancient Jewish Talmud writings state that the taste of the manna was linked to the taster's thoughts.[5]

Think of that: manna provided whatever taste you cared for, simply by imagining it. Feel like a cheeseburger? Your manna tastes like a Whopper. Craving cookies? Voilà, your manna is Oreo flavored. Are you beginning to see that the people's thoughts were the key to what they received in the desert?

Part of the discipline inherent in the manna was its one-day shelf life. They were supposed to gather only enough for each person from the abundance left by the dew. Josephus says that almost inevitably some obeyed their fear and hoarded, but when they had gathered more than the proper portion, they had no more than what was needed, "though they had tired themselves more in gathering it, for they found no more than an omer apiece; and the advantage they got by what was superfluous was none."[6] Within twenty-four hours the excess bred worms and rotted, an interesting principle on hoarding repeated elsewhere: "When you brought it home, I blew it away" (Hg 1:9).

By sending the manna to his people each day, God was forcing them to learn how to rely on him. In the desert, they were at his mercy for survival. And yet this lesson speaks to us as well, despite the abundance in our pantry: unless we develop the discipline of turning to God each day for our needs, he may lead us into the desert to remove our own attachments to security and comfort.

So you need to ask yourself, "Am I willing to trust his divine invisibility every day, or not?" Will I take matters into my own hands, even if it means overextending myself with credit, to provide what I need or simply want? Will I complain against him and chafe at his allowing me to lack what I previously enjoyed? How long will it take? How hungry will he let me get? I went hungry one night myself when learning this lesson.

My Massah and Meribah

We were in the Taco Bell drive-through about five or six miles away from our house one humid, summer Saturday evening when my husband made an offhand comment. I stewed for a few moments, thinking, not for the first time, that I had had enough "bitter" criticism from my dad to last me a lifetime and wouldn't tolerate it from my husband, or anyone else, ever again.

We had placed our orders and were pulling around to the pickup window when my outrage rose up into my chest. I got out of the car and started walking, already planning my retaliatory assault for when he pulled up beside me to apologize and convince me to get back into the car: it was dangerous for a young woman to walk alone through that busy shopping area in the evening, after all.

I was too proud to look back and see how closely he was probably following me, but it didn't matter. I was going to teach him a lesson, and I wouldn't back down no matter how sweetly or thoroughly he proclaimed the error of his ways.

After about five minutes passed, I still didn't see him, and I wondered if he had been held up in the line. Determined not to check, I hiked into the evening shadows that crept over town as the streetlights blinked on and tried to decide if the quickest way home was the back roads or the highway. Since the solitary back roads seemed more dangerous, I started up the ramp, unaware that it was illegal for me to walk on the interstate.

I was probably two miles into my wounded march when I began to question the wisdom of what I had done; cars shot by me at top speed, blowing my hair into my sweaty face; somebody honked at me, and I hunched over as I hurried through the exhaust fumes swirling over me with the wind of passing cars. Once I got off the highway, I still had about four miles to go to reach home.

When I finally made it to our house, it was fully dark, and I was hot, sweaty, hungry, and scared. I headed around to the back door, hoping to avoid my husband. I was too tired and embarrassed to fight and didn't want to talk about my stupidity anyway. Shocked to find him sitting on the back deck in the dark, I brushed past without saying anything and went inside to shower and go to bed.

The next morning, we got ready and drove to church with barely a word between us. The wisdom of his silence was not lost on me when a clueless church member stopped us in the vestibule and all but hollered in my face, "Hey! Did I see you on the interstate last night? I blew the horn at you! What were you doing out there?" I was Peter when the cock crowed, denying my guilt, but my vociferous denials were met with her insistence: "I swear that was your hair I saw!" I hurried to a pew and sat beside my husband, a flood of embarrassment and shame coloring my cheeks. *Bold-faced lying in church. Way to go, Sonja.*

This was not the first time I had embarrassed myself with irrational anger. Sadly, it wouldn't be the last, either. An unresolved father wound kept erupting like a volcano, making it difficult for me to trust in God's love through my husband. Like the Israelites who kept erupting with fear and doubt against God, I continued to erupt in aggressive accusatory tantrums while battling thoughts of worthlessness and a fear of rejection.[7]

By drawing me into the desert, God was inviting me to do the deeper work needed for real rest. I was afraid of God and did not trust him with my deepest hurts and dreams, but God worked with me just as he did with the Israelites, teaching me to see the bitter fruit of my negative thoughts and perceptions, as well as the deeper emotions driving them. And like he did with the Israelites, God used my daily needs to teach me—a little at a time—to trust him and show me how completely he loves me.

Without the Israelites' example to follow and learn from, I am convinced that I would have continued in immature outbursts, manifesting the abandonment I feared most through my behavior, and lost the great gifts of my husband and children, if not literally, then emotionally and spiritually. My irrational behavior in the Taco Bell drive-through was about far more than tacos. I was all but starving for unconditional love and safety yet completely unable to receive all the abundance God was already offering me through my husband and family because I was focusing continually on what was painful, negative, and (imagined as) offensive.

Pay attention to your desert thirsts and hungers. What are you really thirsty and hungry for? Resist the temptation to satisfy yourself, and turn instead to the possibilities in desert emptiness. Ask God for what you need and withstand the discomfort as long as it takes for him to provide for you. He will, even if he has to send angels to do it.

Our Super Substance

It is no accident that after forty days of fasting in the desert, Jesus was also tempted with hunger (Mt 4:1–2). Would Jesus take his hunger into his own hands, using divine power to satisfy himself by turning stones to bread, or would he wait as long as it took for God to provide?

Unlike Israel, who doubted God would provide for their needs in the wilderness and complained against him in their hunger, Jesus did not waver in trusting the Father to provide for him. He was also fed miraculously from heaven (by angels), thereby redeeming another major fall of Israel in the desert. But Jesus does more than overcome Israel's fall; through his victory he makes the desert fruitful for all, so that there is always dew-bread in the desert.

In his person, Jesus is the fulfillment of what the Old Testament manna signified or pointed to: the bread of life from heaven. He taught us to pray for this daily provision: "Give us this day our daily bread" (Mt 6:11). While we wait on God's provision for our physical needs, he provides daily manna in the Eucharist, and with it, grace to persevere in the deprivation.

Why did Jesus teach us to say, "Give us *this day* our *daily* bread"? Aren't "this day" and "daily" redundant? In the Greek they are two different terms. "This day" means *today*, while "daily" is *epiousia* in Greek: *epi-* meaning over, above, super; and *-ousia* meaning existence, essence, subsistence. He means supersubstantial bread (Vulgate), super-being bread, hyperessence bread. He means the Eucharist, as the Church Fathers near unanimously agree. And the Church has long referred to the eucharistic meal itself as "the bread of angels" (*panis angelicus*).

The terms *epiousia*, or *super-essence*, bring to my mind the idea of quantum nonlocality, or quantum reality. As space looks empty, the "daily" bread looks just like normal bread, but under the surface of both is a hyperreality full of infinite possibility requiring only thought to bring it forward.

Disposition Matters

If it is true that the thoughts of the Israelites affected the flavor of the manna, how does my disposition going into Mass affect my ability to receive the graces of the Eucharist into my soul and life? Am I distracted or doubtful about Jesus being truly present? Am I complaining in my heart over the things I lack or have lost? When life presents me opportunities to exercise faith in the guise of needs, do I accept these moments as God's provision for me to see, smell, and taste the sweetness all around me at every moment so that the mysterious, daily miracle does not become empty?

Could it be that God deliberately removes what we previously enjoyed, allowing temporary deprivation in order to reveal a deeper gift and reality? Think of a time when you were unable to receive Jesus in the Eucharist, such as when churches were closed during the pandemic. How much more precious did Jesus become to you when at last you were able to return to the sacraments?

I remember experiencing this in my own life just before the lockdowns, after years of homeschooling schedules that made a daily thirty-mile round trip into town unreasonable. I had finally been able to begin attending daily Mass. I enjoyed the privilege for a little over two months before public Masses ceased due to COVID-19. But there are people I know and admire for it who had been daily communicants for more than a decade. What a beautiful, sacred habit! Surely God understands the value of such a practice, and the absolute necessity Mass is for his people! How could he allow us to go without the Eucharist? Were we being punished? Was the government or Church hierarchy to blame?

We are bound by the sacraments; God is not (*CCC* 1257). Without considering all the other ways we were desolated—isolated, lonely, in financial straits, experiencing health dangers, and scared for our whole world—simply reflect on the fact that he allowed the removal of the Eucharist through means that released us from any guilt, yet still left us separated from him in a way we had never experienced before. Why?

Could it be that, as Christians in the West, (1) we all take the Eucharist for granted, (2) many of the faithful have been praying for the purification of the Church, and (3) a great many Catholics believe going to weekly or daily Mass makes them holy, in and of itself, regardless of what their thoughts, motives, dispositions, attachments, and habits might be? Did God want to remind us all that weekly and even daily Mass is meant to fortify the deeper work of releasing deeply rooted unforgiveness, inordinate attachments and dependencies, negative thoughts and dark emotions, and "little" idolatries? Do you see how even a beautiful, sacred habit can sometimes become an impediment to deeper trust and purity in our love for God? For all these reasons, a vast desert might be a necessary spiritual discipline.

If I rely on morning prayer, and for whatever reason that possibility disappears, I am forced to find another, unfamiliar prayer routine. Do I prefer unhealthy isolation? Circumstances may arise to force me into community. Do I engage in spiritual activity as a distraction or as a measure of holiness? I may soon find myself inactive. Do I grasp at comfort in relationships? I may suddenly experience isolation or alienation. Do I draw my identity or security from my job? I may experience some kind of transition or opposition; I may even lose my job.

In the desert God removes the comforts and props—however holy they may be—on which we have become dependent. He strips them away, one by one or all at once, until it seems there is nothing left, allowing deprivations that force us to grope for and find him in different (licit) ways. For example, many people who were unable to receive the Eucharist during the pandemic began seeking God and finding him in the scriptures for the first time. Although frustrating and often confusing, this desert way of "changing things up" is a hallmark of God's activity and purification, according to the doctors of prayer. This is the essence of purgatory, *and we are meant to do it here, in the desert,* where we have access to the sacraments, science, prayer, and medicine to assist us in the difficulties.

St. Teresa of Avila's *The Interior Castle*, St. John of the Cross's *Ascent of Mount Carmel* and *Dark Night of the Soul*, James Fowler's *Stages of Faith*, and Rev. Reginald Garrigou-Lagrange's *The Three Ages of the Interior Life* all describe the paradox of the Holy Spirit's rest-giving desert ways—the process of purging our attachments so we will learn to rely solely on his indwelling presence and Word, which is truly the only unassailable reality. How we respond in this deprivation determines whether we move beyond it or experience further pop quizzes in the same theme. The Israelites' accusations reveal their deep-seated suspicion of God and fear of dying in the desert, and it does not seem that miraculous water or food made them grateful or helped them place more faith in God rather than their fear. So the pop quizzes kept coming.

Recognizing Desert Distractions

God had fulfilled the promise by his own hand; the community of Israel had arrived at the edge of Canaan, the promised land. The narrator (Moses) seems impressed with the Lord's timing, pointing out their arrival as three months to the day of the Exodus (Ex 19:1). Water for themselves and their flocks was supernaturally provided from the rock that followed them through the desert (1 Cor 10:4); they had been fed for three months on the miraculous dew-manna. Their daily needs were met by the tender hand of God himself, but the people would not rest in the desert uncertainty, despite proof after proof of God's provision, despite satiated thirst and full bellies. They created a diversion to distract themselves from dealing with the root of their unrest. The next momentous events would shape their subsequent history forever.

Moses ascended Mount Sinai in a covenant-making ceremony, where he stayed for forty days (see Exodus 19:3–25). Something glorious was being "born" on that mountain, but his extended absence and the terrifying setting into which he had disappeared led the people to suspect all they feared for themselves, that he might never return. After so long a wait, they spoke of his absence in sarcastic, scathing terms: "This Moses . . ." (see Exodus

32:1). The Acts of the Apostles editorializes, "In their hearts they turned to Egypt" (7:39).

Assuming abandonment, they convinced Aaron to fashion a golden calf for them to worship. He used the rich Egyptian jewelry from the treasure intended for use in building and furnishing the worship tabernacle that would draw them into intimacy with God.[8] What followed was considered forever after as one of the two most scandalous episodes in Israelite history—profane worship of a gold idol involving orgiastic immorality—a "great sin" (Ex 32:30), a road to further difficulties, and a gross impediment to all the blessing God desired to give them.

Believing they had been abandoned and failing to trust, the Israelites worshiped a pagan Egyptian deity at the foot of the mountain where both God and Moses were present the entire time. The Israelites seem almost manic in their search for diversion while waiting in the desert, partying with bovine Egyptian and Canaanite gods of wealth, fertility, and power. In a sinister summary of the debacle, the Bible says simply, "And the people sat down to eat and drink, and rose up to play" (Ex 32:6).

When I am in my own desert and feeling deprived, what diversion or comfort-seeking measure do I turn to for relief, and what are the consequences of those forms of escapism? How much time have I wasted pursuing destructive habits, time that I can never get back? What relationships have I damaged, and whom have I hurt in my need for distraction? What counterfeit "golden calves" have I embraced in pursuit of genuine intimacy?

The desert reveals the illusory nature of comfort and prosperity, self-sufficiency and control. We cling stubbornly to these illusions at times, lying to ourselves that if we relinquish these trappings we will perish in the desert. When our dryness, loneliness, dependency, barrenness, lack of control, and fear are exposed, the reality can be almost unbearable. Emotional pressure mounts, and we rush to anesthetize ourselves from the reality of our condition to assuage the anxiety we feel. Comfort seeking takes hold. And in the distraction of providing outward satiation for ourselves, we may become incapable of receiving the promise altogether.

When we do not seem to be making progress in an endeavor—especially in the desert, where difficulties are multiplied—the temptation is always to distract ourselves from the sense of possible futility and failure. But that's the worst time and place to give ourselves up to distractions, primarily because we take our eyes off the "real thing," the Presence in the emptiness that waits for us to approach him with our deepest desires and needs for intimacy.

Focusing on the Real Thing

Jesus knew focusing on diversions could never come close to the love that sustains the universe, the real thing.

On the Mount of Temptation, Satan tempted Jesus to distraction with worldly kingdoms and all their fickle admiration, influence, and ease. Jesus refused to turn attention away from his desert purpose, direction, and communion with the Father, where true intimacy is found. He responded by speaking his immovable trust in the first of the Ten Commandments and quoting Deuteronomy 6:13: "You shall worship the Lord your God, and him only shall you serve" (Mt 4:8).

At its most basic, worship is love. Do we love the world and seek intimacy in diversions and empty idolatries, such as power, porn, or addiction (including socially sanctioned, "harmless" forms such as Instagram and Facebook followers, shopping, gambling, or drinking)? Or do we go to God with our raw need for love, intimacy, and desire? The desert will reveal it.

In this third temptation, Jesus overcame Israel's sin of idolatry, winning for all the grace to resist distraction while experiencing deprivation; for the gravest temptations come when we are most afraid that all is lost, and yet that is also often when we are at the threshold of the promise.

Graves of Craving

After the incident with the golden calf, the Lord withdrew his presence on Mount Sinai, and would have removed his protection and guidance from the Israelites permanently had Moses not intervened. Still, the consequences of their sin were not removed but postponed; their desert was extended another thirty-eight futile years, and none of those who had fallen in sinful distraction would make it in (Ex 32:33–35). When after two years they were meant to enter, we discover why God's prediction was true: their lust for diversion from their desert purpose had multiplied and led to a more sinister poison, one that became permanently clear in the "graves of craving" (Nm 11:34).

This name comes from an incident at Tab'erah (or "the burning," see Nm 11:3), in which the people continued to complain of a strong "craving" (lust) for variety in their diet, for meat, just as they had craved distraction with the false idol of gold. God allowed their craving to "consume" the people, whose lack of gratitude, satisfaction, and willingness to work more deeply than their superficial needs had caused them time and again to turn away from him rather than toward him.

Within sight of the breathtaking plenitude and variety of the promised land, they whined like toddlers, "O that we had meat to eat! We remember the fish we ate in Egypt for nothing, the cucumbers, the melons, the leeks, the onions, and the garlic; but now our strength is dried up, and there is nothing at all but this manna to look at" (Nm 11:5–6).

Moses was discouraged to the point of death at the prospect that he should somehow provide meat for the multitude. The Israelites grumbled and wailed in exaggeration that their souls were "dried up" from deprivation of rich food while standing mere feet from the indescribable buffet of the promised land! This is the ultimate danger of refusing to submit to the lessons of the desert: desolation in a land of plenty. The miraculous manna had grown monotonous, even worthless, to them. Refusing to eat it another day, they were willing to reject freedom and return to slavery rather than confront their deeper need, even at the threshold of the promised land flowing with milk and honey.

God heard them: migrating coveys of quail fluttered by the millions into the camp on the wind. The people's frenzied craving at a peak, they gorged themselves literally to death on wild game (Nm 11:33). The people's hysteria consumed them at the precipice of the promise. Thousands died, and the place was named *Kibroth Hattaavah*, meaning "graves of craving." What they devoured, devoured them.

The Cause of Purposelessness

Think of a time when you undertook an endeavor that was soon beset with continual setbacks and multiplied frustrations, pushing you to the breaking point of giving up in disgust. What wouldn't you have given to overcome this creeping sense of failure? How many times have you personally experienced that "distractions breed destruction," a time when an intense craving for something got out of hand and devoured you? Isn't this the very definition of addiction?

Not long ago I asked God if I could have something, and was startled when he said, "Are you sure?" I thought about the Israelites dying for meat next door to more abundance than they could ever consume in a lifetime. I was suddenly sure I didn't want it anymore, even though I had no idea why. My prayer became, "Lord, if what I request prevents you from giving me something better than I asked for, please cancel my request!" The Israelites easily could have had a similar exchange with God. I am thankful their example is in the Bible and that the warnings to heed it are so fervent: the strongest temptations in the desert are often those within sight of the promised land.

On the surface, desert complaints seem legitimate. No one can live without food and water. No one could blame the Israelites for wanting meat to eat. All of these events—Marah, Massah and Meribah, manna, carnal distraction, quail—all beg the following question: If sustenance, intimacy, and leisure are all human needs, and God says he will provide for all our needs, why did God judge them for their "cravings"?

Psalm 78 sheds more light on the graves of craving event:

> They ate and were well filled,
>   for he gave them what they craved. . . .
> In spite of all this they still sinned;
>   despite his wonders they did not believe. (78:29,
>   32)

We learn that "they ate and were well filled" unto judgment because of their unbelief. The book of Wisdom teaches it this way: "One is punished by the very things by which he sins" (Ws 11:16). Every discomfort in the desert became an opportunity to suspect God's motives and find fault with him. And so, while the quail was in their mouths, it was judgment that they swallowed, for they had refused to address the root of their furious greed and consumption: "Their days He consumed in futility, and their years *in fear*" (Ps 78:33 NKJV, emphasis added).

This is a dire warning. The people who fell to diversion at the foot of Mount Sinai were so driven by buried fears that they poisoned themselves with delicacies and died directly outside the promised land *with the same bitter fear that they harbored in their hearts upon leaving Egypt.* Those who didn't succumb to death were too afraid of the giants in the land to enter it, too focused on negativity, and too undisciplined to trust God for rest.

The Israelites' residual fear drove them to distraction and away from rest and plenitude; therefore they could not enter the promised land. Rather than facing their fear and receiving the promise, they received every awful thing they continually anguished over. They had not learned the desert ways that lead to rest. In following God, we must understand that a fog of urgency surrounds deprivations; we must never trust barren circumstances. Rather, we must determine to believe what God says in his Word, trust his limitless possibility, his goodness, and his provision.

The people could not receive rest in sweet water, in abundant water, in daily manna, in the quiet boredom of a temporary absence, or in the peace of waiting just a few more days for excitement and variety beyond their wildest dreams. A change in scenery made no difference; even when camped at the boundary of the promised land, they still would not rest. Despite pop quiz after pop quiz, they chose again and again to reject the lesson God was trying to teach them. The people would never rest, would never find release. They clung to stubborn, negative, fearful thinking and continued to receive negativity and fear until they died.

As I struggled in my own desert, I realized something important: for the two years that the Israelites wandered in the wilderness, they were never more than a week's walk away from the promised land. And what was true of them, is true for us as well. No matter how far into the desert I wander, the promised land is always closer than it feels, so long as I keep moving forward.

The promised land really is as close as my determination to confront fear and negativity head-on with the Holy Spirit. As I have disciplined my thoughts with the truth of God's Word, set my will toward my promise and resolved to go "all the way" with God, no matter what that entailed, every persistent, glorious step of victory in following God's Word has been rewarded more plentifully than I ever dreamed.

Do you feel purposeless, empty, and unsatisfied? Are you living in pervasive anxiety or fear? Do you continually accuse others, yourself, or God of a lack of variety or insufficiency? Have you demanded and received, rather than resting in God's perfect provision for you or asking him in simple, quiet, trusting faith for what you need or want? Are you focusing on deficits and drawing more of them to yourself through complaints and negativity?

According to the scriptures, when we refuse to address our lingering fear, negativity, doubt, and faithlessness in the desert, we begin to wander in purposelessness. It is people who go astray in their hearts and do not know God's ways that follow this well-worn path. The Israelites never talked with God about the bitterness and residual fear with which their slavery in Egypt had left them, and they missed the promised land of rest completely.

A Residual Fear of Cancer

Remember my friend who asked for prayer about an ultrasound and biopsy for breast cancer? She watched her own mother develop and suffer from breast cancer, and a great trepidation lurked and grew in her heart. Memories of her mother were clouded by this fear and foreboding because of the devastating effects of the disease on her body. The ultrasound and biopsy her doctor ordered after a routine mammogram brought all of this fear raging to the surface.

What should we do in these moments? Is it really hopeless? Could something wonderful be trying to happen . . . even in such awful, fearful moments?

I suggested to my friend that she notice the lessons of the children of Israel in the desert: focusing consistently on something has a way of drawing it to you. By continually focusing on her mother's cancer, my friend had unconsciously focused her thoughts on that fear and negativity for years. *Everyone* subconsciously focuses on what they fear, often drawing that very thing into their lives. Of course, this does not mean we are to "blame" for awful things like cancer. Rather, the key is to become aware that's what we've been doing (if we have) and address the fear directly and honestly, getting it out in the open where God can heal and transform it, rather than allowing it to operate subconsciously and metastasize through fear.

As we explored her difficult relationship with her own mother, my friend exclaimed, "I realize now that I have been burying many fears. I stuff them. I have stuffed my fear of cancer and death! I didn't know what to do with it."

Together, we addressed years of negative thoughts and fear in God's presence and with his help. I shared two techniques that helped her immerse herself in God and regain her peace, techniques I will share with you. When she realized how deeply God wanted to heal her and experienced his transformation of her long-held secret fears and anger, she was amazed by the new strength and lightness she felt; she was excited by the realities he had opened up before her. The process had been temporarily painful, yes, but it was a *welcome* suffering because it led straight to rest in places she had never been able to rest before.

Higher Thought: The Mind of Christ

The Israelites existed in and were connected to the Source of all that is, and because God was present with them throughout their desert journey, water and food were always available—twelve wells, water from a rock, manna from heaven with the dew. Even so, fear veiled this reality and prevented them from seeing that they were literally surrounded by all they needed. Their focus, fears, and ungrateful thoughts were always on what they lacked rather than the desert possibilities.

What are your desert possibilities?

I speak of lower faith rather than the theological virtue when I say this: thought creates faith, and faith creates everything. Like divine love, the gift of divine faith is higher than the superficial faith we operate in most of the time, and that's why we need the desert to reveal the difference. Because the Israelites' thoughts were on their fear, their *faith* was in their fear—they *believed* their fear—and fear is what they received: they drew more of what they feared to themselves by giving it traction in their minds and hearts—by *expecting* it. This is the lower faith, often unconscious, that most of us operate in the majority of the time. The desert is meant to draw us to higher consciousness, divine faith that honestly acknowledges fear and deprivations and trusts God through them.

We all know exhausting, toxic people who are always thinking about all that can go wrong. No matter what good comes their way, they dwell on doom and destruction, and always think the grass is greener on the other side. They seem to be magnets for drama and conflict. As a result of all of this negative and morbid thinking, nothing ever makes them happy or content because nothing is ever good enough. People who are not happy and fulfilled, who are always pessimistic and depressed, and have negative attitudes toward everybody and everything, *choose* to think and dwell on negativity. A million daily Masses and Bible studies will offer you dew, but they will not overrule your free will!

Negative thinking is lower consciousness based in survival and protection. The choice *not* to think negative thoughts will cause them to fade.[9] Then we are free to think higher thoughts in health and wisdom, where God's thoughts and ways are. We have been given this power over our thinking: "We have the mind of Christ" (1 Cor 2:16). You *can* "be transformed by the renewal of your mind" (Rom 12:2). Controlling your thoughts is absolutely necessary for rest. Our circumstances may not change at all, but we can rest perfectly in the midst of them.

Restful Counterfeits

Some people hear me say that God has given us power over our thinking and make false assumptions about what I mean by this. Let me clear up a few of these "restful counterfeits," right out of the gate.

When I talk about resting in God and having positive thoughts, I don't mean psyching yourself up with wishful thinking, with something that you don't really believe deep down: that's actually adding lies to disbelief.

I am not advancing the simplistic "power of positive thinking" or "name it and claim it" theology. God is not a celestial gumball machine—you can't put in a prayer and automatically get out what you want. Our heavenly Father knows and gives what is best for us.

Finally, I am not advocating denying the reality of poverty, sickness, or suffering. It would be foolish to say, "Diabetes be gone," and indiscriminately stop taking your prescribed medications; the Bible does not at all advocate this, and neither do I. Rather, we should take care of our bodies and follow our doctor's advice.

On the other hand, if we trust God's promise of rest and say, "I can be healthy," and act on that belief—by maintaining a healthy weight, mitigating stress, exercising, and guarding against negative, disease-creating thoughts—if we act and keep acting on our faith, it is possible to recover our health to a great degree, if not completely.

Disciplining one's thoughts is about more than positive thinking; it's about trusting God's Word over our own fears. God promises to provide for our needs. When I need something in the desert, I should discern with the Holy Spirit what that *really* is, ask him for it, and wait as long as it takes for him to provide it while exhausting all the options available to me—not pretend I am happy about not having it!

For the same reason, I want to reiterate that having difficulties and dis-ease does not make us to blame for them. Do you see how blame and judgment continue the cycle of negativity and fear rather than bringing it to God for healing? We become obsessed with thinking positive thoughts that are not actually true. Thinking, "I must be positive," when you truly feel scared or angry is simply suppressing reality and compounding the destruction of the negativity and fear. Instead, we must acknowledge and accept and love the absolute truth of ourselves—fear, negativity, and all. We'll talk about how to do that at the end of this chapter and in the next, but for now it is enough to acknowledge that desert deprivations provoke such fears precisely so we can carry those burdens and worries to Jesus.

Disciplined Thinking Leads to Rest

As they wandered in the desert, as the Israelites allowed undisciplined negative thoughts to rule, they sowed in fear and reaped more fear. They brought the bitterness of Egypt to Marah, and the water was too bitter to drink. Their thoughts determined the taste of the manna, and it became "worthless" and withered their souls. They thought God was too selfish to give them variety and spice, and they ate themselves to death in boredom.

Seven times the original narrative says the Israelites complained and wept over temporary deprivations and unsatisfactory provisions. Seven times they accused God of intending to kill them in the desert. Over and over what erupts from their mouths shows us their thoughts. They repeatedly experienced circumstances meant to teach them to confront their fears and trust God's provision and timing, but the people never learned. Instead, they continued receiving all they expected, all they were thinking, and all they gave voice to.

Rest in Thought

Intelligence is part of what it means to bear the image of God and be cocreators with him. "Each of us is the result of a thought of God. Each of us is willed, each of us is loved, each of us is necessary," Pope Benedict XVI asserted.[10] Just as God's thought or "observation" brought the universe into being and keeps it in existence, just as a scientist's observation determines whether light energy appears as particle or wave, we also bring to being what we have trained our minds to observe, or focus on, through our thoughts. Concentrated, consistent thought *happens*. Archbishop Fulton Sheen put it this way: "Man is good and tells the secret of his goodness in the language of thought."[11]

What we think about and how we think about it become reality. The Bible is full of this idea, once you attend to it. Scripture reveals what science reflects, that our thoughts create actions or inactions, and that those actions or inactions create outcomes or circumstances. For instance,

- "Whatever you ask in prayer, you will receive, if you have faith" (Mt 21:22).
- "Be transformed by the renewal of your mind, that you may prove what is the will of God" (Rom 12:2).
- "Take every thought captive to obey Christ" (2 Cor 10:5).
- "Keep your heart with all vigilance; for from it flow the springs of life" (Prv 4:23).
- "The good man out of the good treasure of his heart produces good, and the evil man out of his evil treasure produces evil; for out of the abundance of the heart his mouth speaks" (Lk 6:45).

- "Faith is the realization of what is hoped for and evidence of things not seen" (Heb 11:1, NAB).

Thought is a type of *energy*. The first law of thermodynamics maintains that energy can never be destroyed; it can only change form. Energy can be altered to a different kind of energy, but it can never be annihilated—it always exists somewhere in some form.

Similarly, thoughts are spiritual energy that is never lost and can never be destroyed. Thoughts are powerful because they create. Negative thoughts and fears must be challenged and transformed so they no longer create destruction. The primary way we transform negative thoughts and fears is by trusting in the truth of God's Word. Once negative thoughts and fears are transformed, they become the life-producing energy of love.

Because all things exist in God, all things are possible with God (Mt 19:26). Our thoughts of faith and possibility connect us in prayer to the One who upholds the entire cosmos together and in whom exist all possibilities. If my thoughts are in fear, deprivation, and negativity, I get fear, deprivation, and negativity. Your thoughts bring things into being. "Make no mistake: God is not mocked, for a person will reap only what he sows" (Gal 6:7, NAB).

What about death and tragedy? How do you think positively when the person you love most in the world is wasting away before your eyes, when your heart bleeds with sorrow and shatters to pieces with pain? We cannot and must not "be strong," psyching ourselves up in the face of evil and tragedy. We must always live in truth. Pretending, even to ourselves, betrays the truth. It is a lie to pretend to be happy or positive when we are dying inside. And sometimes the unrest is so deep we don't even know where it comes from.

Acknowledge the truth of what you *really* feel. Look for the positive, the dew, in your sorrow. Ask God to show it to you if you cannot see it. The Bible promises when we ask for wisdom, God's perspective, he will always give it to us (Jas 1:5). Always seek God's perspective on your circumstances, because negativity really is about perspective. Understanding circumstances from

God's point of view, which is always love, gives you the gift to cling to in the worst suffering and trouble, the dew that gets you through one more step.

Thoughts may be insistent, and we might almost obsess over them, but we can and should become a part of the creative, healing process by diverting our thoughts to "whatever is true, whatever is honorable, whatever is just, whatever is pure, whatever is lovely, whatever is gracious, if there is any excellence, if there is anything worthy of praise" (Phil 4:8).

Besides the scriptures, an important way to change our thoughts is through gratitude. Gratitude focuses on the positive. And gratitude is a magnet for miracles. How can we observe daily dew with thanksgiving if we aren't looking for it? Ending each day with the daily Ignatius examen is a gentle tool for cultivating conscious gratitude. The daily examen is a prayerful reflection on the events of the day in order to detect God's presence, discern his direction, and gather the day's dew in gratitude. A simple version of the examen is to become aware of God's presence; review the day with gratitude; acknowledge your thoughts and emotions; pick something from the day to pray from, something you might improve or something you did well; and look forward to tomorrow. Practicing daily gratitude is holy antiseptic for infected thought habits.

For forty years God provided the Israelites with absolutely everything they needed to reach the promised land. Neither their shoes nor their clothes wore out in all that time (Dt 29:5), and had they learned the lessons of the desert, they would have had all they needed to prosper there. St. Paul goes so far as to say that their stubbornness in refusing to learn the desert lessons, and the refusal of following generations to learn them as well, are what caused their failure to recognize their Messiah.[12]

It is hard to trust when you're scared, I know, but fear is "evil unbelief," according to our text in Hebrews, because it leads away from God, the Source. The only way to learn that God is trustworthy is to trust him in deprivations. Take him at his Word, step out in faith, and act on what he says. "I give you everything"

(Gn 9:3). "You are always with me, and all that is mine is yours" (Lk 15:31). He sends dew at every step. When we trust God's provision and we trust God's timing, we experience rest, even in deprivation. This is the faith that makes fruitful, the love that creates. This is the promised land of rest in our thoughts.

Let's Review

Let's review how to find rest in our worries.

- The Holy Spirit warns us repeatedly not to rebel against desert deprivations, but to seek God's provision and trust in his timing.
- Worries are tests of trust, but needs are not punishment. Needs are an invitation to experience God's love and provision, and to overcome our bondage to fear and bitterness.
- God will always provide what I need from the infinite possibilities of who he is.
- Daily manna falls with the dew. I receive the graces to help me navigate the desert fruitfully in the Eucharist, my "daily bread," with the proper disposition of faith and trust.
- The deprivations I experience in the desert—the removal of spiritual "props"—are intended to lead me to seek God elsewhere.
- Yielding to desert distractions prolongs my desert and causes me to forfeit the rest I crave.
- The Israelites' experience in the desert reminds me I must honestly acknowledge my fears in order to enter the promised land of rest.
- In the desert, God will expose and heal my bitterness and fear so he can transform them, as long as I bring these things to him honestly.
- Disciplined thinking leads to rest.
- I discipline my thinking through the truth of the Word of God.

An Invitation

The most effective way to change fearful, negative thoughts, a process which can greatly benefit both the brain and body, is through prayer,[13] especially praying the scriptures. Andrew Newberg, a neuroscientist at the University of Pennsylvania, has studied the mental and physiological effects of prayer. He is a pioneer in the neurological study of religious and spiritual experiences, a rapidly growing field known as neurotheology.

Speaking of prayer, Newberg states, "When people are engaged in practices over a long period of time, it does ultimately alter how the person's brain functions. . . . As one does a particular practice or a particular task over and over, that becomes more and more written into the neural connections of the brain. So the more you focus on something . . . the more that becomes your reality."[14]

The more you focus on love, the more you become love. When we find ourselves in the desert, focusing on the negative only draws more negativity. But daily prayer in the scriptures corrects negative, fearful thoughts with the truth of God's Word. Often, we don't have proper perspective on our circumstances because we are functioning from the fog of urgency, fear, and negativity. Diving deep into scripture is primary in combating the lies that the enemy tells us, to truly know who God is and what he wants for us and from us. The sacraments are powerful sources of strength and healing, but they are only a portion of the equation. Part of the "one table" of the Lord that includes both the Eucharist and the scriptures (*CCC* 103–4), the Word of God offers the clear self-knowledge and understanding that are absolutely necessary for learning to rest in our thoughts.

Bringing our worries and fears to God in prayer with the scriptures on a daily basis through LOVE the Word is daily dew. God is speaking every day through the daily readings of the Church about my desert, my deprivations and worries. In the scriptures, the Holy Spirit helps us focus on the innumerable possibilities in God and work toward those. Ask, "Where is the water?" Pray, "Lead me to water, Lord." Sink into the connectedness inherent in all things and draw on him and the dew available in the scripture readings. The road will rise up to meet you, as they say, because God always responds to faith with provision. He has written this sowing-and-reaping principle in spiritual law. "God is not man, that he should lie. . . . Has he said, and will he not do it? Or has he spoken, and will he not fulfil it?" (Nm 23:19).

Benediction—LOVE the Word

Throughout your reading in this chapter, the Holy Spirit likely drew your attention to an area or areas of deprivation, worry, and unrest in your life. Perhaps your worst fear leaped to the surface. Maybe your thoughts made your breathing difficult and your heart pound. Acknowledge all you are thinking and feeling. Your awareness is his invitation for you to experience his love in these areas.

For a few moments, remembering you are in his presence and that he holds you in his unspeakable love, list these fears with him. Imagine your worst fear, the one that harasses you in unguarded moments. Maybe it's the loss of a child or loved one, or maybe it's something else entirely, but allow your mind to go there, all the way there, to your absolute worst fear. Imagine every event, every step, all you might feel or think, were it to happen.

Perhaps you do not have to imagine at all. Maybe you have lived through this trauma personally. What do you want to say to God? What are your fears?

L | Listen (Receive the Word.)

As you repeat the following verse in his presence, try personalizing it and emphasizing each word or phrase in turn. Ask him to speak to your heart very clearly through this verse. You might try it like this, from Philippians 4:19:

"*My* God will supply every need of yours according to his riches in glory."

"My *God* will supply every need of yours according to his riches in glory."

"My God *will* supply every need of yours according to his riches in glory."

"My God will *supply* every need of yours according to his riches in glory."

"My God will supply *every* need of yours according to his riches in glory."

Continue emphasizing each word or phrase in turn until you have focused on them all.

O | Observe (Observe your relationships and circumstances.)

Is there any fear or need that you could possibly have that is not addressed in this verse? Do you trust that what God says in his Word is absolutely true? What has God said to you through this chapter, and what does this verse say to you about unrest and fear in your relationships and the events in your life right now?

V | Verbalize (Pray through your thoughts and emotions.)

Lord, I am frequently afraid of and worry about . . .
    Lord, I need . . .
    But what if . . .

E | Entrust (May it be done to me according to your word.)

Lord, I receive. Lord, I believe. Help my unbelief. Amen.

As one with a father wound, I had no rest, even when I was still. I lived in fear of worthlessness and emotional abandonment, especially by God, that spewed out in a destructive, sinful pattern of dark, ugly thoughts and raging emotional eruptions. I tried to conquer the cycle of negative thoughts, and I gained a measure of success, but was still sometimes bewildered and conquered by them instead. It was time to go deeper than my thoughts. The Lord led me further into the Israelite desert and far deeper into my own soul than I fathomed could exist.

Three

EMOTIONS AT REST

Conquering the Desert

[The Lord said . . .] "Now therefore arise, go over this Jordan, you and all this people, into the land which I am giving to them. . . . Every place that the sole of your foot will tread upon I have given to you."

—Joshua 1:2, 3

Years after writing that first study and many afterward, my promise remained unfulfilled. I was no closer to being published than I had been at the beginning of the desert. Far from the plenitude I felt I had been promised, I had been forced to take a part-time job as a church secretary to help make ends meet. I was seething with anger over the rebellion of the church members that had split our church and sent me wandering in denominational emptiness and spiritual darkness. I had not yet found rest. But the dew kept falling.

One morning I was reading in the fifth chapter of Joshua. The Israelites had just encountered their first enemy stronghold. Jericho had to be defeated in order to proceed into the land. Joshua encounters a "man" with his sword drawn and asks him, "Are you for us, or for our adversaries?" (5:13).

As I read that question, I began to think of the agitators at my former church. *Yeah!* I said to the Lord. *Whose side are you on, here, anyway? They're in blatant sin!*

The answer was, simply, noncommittally, *No* (5:14).

"Whose side are you on?"

"No."

At first I was astonished, and then irritated. I mean, why would God not be on the "right" side or clearly against the side of evil? As I thought about the situation at church, it seemed like God was holding me to a higher standard, dragging me off through the desert while leaving those who had all but destroyed my church "back in Egypt." While I appreciated that he wasn't taking sides, I couldn't help but wonder: *Why had God been correcting my rebellion at every turn for the past decade, and allowing others to get away with even worse behavior?* I had asked for—and received—the graces I needed to overcome such behavior. Why couldn't they? Where was the *justice*?

I resolved to find the answer. There had to be more to it.

Indeed.

A pop quiz approached.

Showers of Dew and Shiny Silver Swans

With this conflict broiling in my heart, I knelt at the foot of an elderly relative's toilet, determinedly scrubbing weeks-old feces out of her pink shag carpet. Aunt Betty was a formidable woman. Fiercely independent and self-sufficient, she was adamant about remaining in her home as long as possible, but it became increasingly difficult for her to get around, and she routinely had accidents while trying to make it to the bathroom.

I had taken on cleaning for Aunt Betty every month in a spirit of, if not real charity, at least Christian duty. I was thankful that her eyesight was probably too weak to notice what I was doing; she would have been embarrassed to find out that anyone had to perform such a task for her. Like most people, the dignified old woman despised her own neediness and could not tolerate pity from others.

Characteristic of her generation, Aunt Betty never asked me to clean her carpet, and to save her the embarrassment of her "weakness" and "neediness" I never mentioned when I did.

Instead, I fumed at the foot of that toilet, scrubbing harder and harder as I thought of the presumption and pride of those gossiping backbiters who had ripped apart God's beloved church.

The angry scrubbing motion felt strangely soothing. As I struggled, God laid a silent question, a subtle challenge, on the altar of my heart: Why are you on your knees, sweating and scouring the foul carpet in front of you?

Shocked, I did not have a ready answer, so I scrubbed and wondered. Why *was* I struggling with that filthy task for a woman to whom I was only remotely related, barely knew, and who had not asked me to do it in the first place?

While the television in the next room blared with court shows and Scooby Doo, the astonishing answer rolled over me the way my son drove Hot Wheels up and down Aunt Betty's legs: I was willing to clean excrement out of her carpet without any sort of acknowledgment of what I had done *because I loved the crusty old woman.* She cussed like a sailor, was cynical to the point of meanness, and rarely had a nice thing to say, yet I had fallen in love with her because in her weakness, she needed me.

As I scoured, my heart soared with the truth of it. How could my reluctant service to this elderly aunt have produced in my heart a truly warm, sacrificial love for her? My memory paraded short, endearing incidents, accumulated over time: the Shoney's fried shrimp she always requested on the way home from shopping; how I had to secretly tip the servers when we went to eat after her doctor's appointments because she always stiffed them; the way she played intensely competitive dominoes and card games with my eight-year-old son while I cleaned; the twenty-year stash of presents under every bed and in every closet, waiting to be regifted. Over time, mutual tolerance had blossomed into genuine regard, then something altogether lovelier. With that thought, I scrubbed a little more zealously, wanting, *needing*, to show her just how much I truly loved her by scrubbing out her weakness.

At that precise moment, the Lord revealed the real lesson. With a single piercing flash, I came to understand that he felt the

same way about those "disgusting" church members as I felt about
Aunt Betty. I realized that their profound weakness, like my own,
likely came from a place of deep woundedness and probably a
sense of worthlessness, too. These deeply rooted emotions moved
the Lord to love them desperately, knowing full well that only
he could ever help them. There on my knees in that bathroom, I
understood in a way that changed me permanently that "mercy
triumphs over judgment" (Jas 2:13).

Dew fell all over me that day at the foot of Aunt Betty's fuch-
sia toilet in the Pepto-Bismol pink bathroom with the shiny silver
swans on the wallpaper and the mauve shag carpet, and I wept.
His mercy had brought me out of the same incontinent rebellion they were in; he had corrected me and placed me on the
right path, without ever breaking the bruised reed of my heart (Is
42:1–3). His mercy preserved a cynical Aunt Betty as a witness
of his tender love, and his mercy showed me how to love those
church members and treat them with the charity and dignity
they deserved.

This, this is justice.

The Supreme Task of Justice

"If we confess our sins, he is faithful and *just*, and will forgive our
sins and cleanse us from all unrighteousness" (1 Jn 1:9, emphasis
added). We are forgiven the sin, cleansed of the deed, and even
the inclination if we pursue forgiveness to its completion: "*all*
unrighteousness." Forgiveness, beloved, is the supreme task of
justice. For God, for you.

Forgiveness does not mean there should be no boundaries
or that there are no consequences. Sin contains its own inherent,
inescapable consequences—for us, for them (see Wisdom 11:16
and Romans 6:23). But as is also true of rest, justice in the social
sphere begins with forgiveness in those family, parish, and other
societal relationships and circumstances that challenge us the
hardest. "Blessed are those who hunger and thirst for righteousness, for they shall be satisfied" (Mt 5:6). The word "righteousness" means "justice"; the words are interchangeable.

What's more, unforgiveness is demonic torment for the one who will not extend it. In speaking on unforgiveness, Jesus taught a parable about an unmerciful servant who had been forgiven an enormous debt, one that could never have been repaid in his entire lifetime (see Matthew 18). The wicked servant then turned to another who owed him a meager debt and threw him in prison when he was unable to repay. The Lord of both servants delivered the wicked servant to the jailers. Most translations use the word *tormentors* or *torturers*. Jesus finishes with, "So also my heavenly Father will do to every one of you, if you do not forgive your brother from your heart" (Mt 18:35). Who are the torturers? To whom are we imprisoned when we withhold the justice of forgiveness? The demons, who prowl the earth seeking souls whom they may devour (see 1 Peter 5:8).

Forgiveness is rarely a onetime endeavor, as Jesus indicated in the same exchange with Peter on forgiveness. We must forgive "seventy times seven" (Mt 18:22), meaning until forgiveness is entirely complete. This requires time, help, and guidance from the Holy Spirit. Every time we are tempted to descend into the rabbit hole of angry, painful memories, we lay our ugly thoughts and emotions at the feet of Jesus and leave the judgment to him. We ask the Holy Spirit if there's anything or anyone left to forgive. Otherwise unforgiveness embroils us in torment, metastasizes in sickness, and erupts in destructive emotional incontinence.

The lack of control that I abhor so desperately in myself, the weakness that provokes all my defenses and denial and pretension, the neediness I hide: these are the weaknesses that draw the Lord closest to me. Clinging to this knowledge, I am increasingly able to beg for grace whenever this weakness is triggered by a hateful "other," and I am suddenly called to control my own instinctive incontinence.

The Strength of Weakness

"Who is weak, and I am not weak? Who is made to fall, and I am not indignant? . . . 'For my power is made perfect in weakness.' I will all the more gladly boast of my weaknesses, that the power of Christ may rest upon me" (2 Cor 11:29, 12:9). Transformed in this light, our most embarrassing indignity becomes the path on which we soar to sanctity. The crusty old woman and our nasty Christian sister and brother become the sweetest allies, our personal escorts to holiness.

As I left Aunt Betty's house that day on a Holy Spirit high, I thought about a hateful church lady who had caused a public, irreconcilable conflict in my church by slandering those who had not supported her views. I had not spoken to her for months, but then and there I prayed for the opportunity to see her and be reconciled with her again. Then, resting in the peace of forgiveness, I promptly forgot about her . . . until I literally ran into her a few weeks later at my son's school.

When we collided in a narrow doorway, we both took a step back in shocked recognition. With a hundred-watt smile I almost shrieked, "I am so glad to see you! How are you?" Before I could say more, she disappeared down the hall. But that was okay; I wasn't even disappointed. I was amazed—and thankful—to discover that the Holy Spirit really had done a work in my heart that day in the ugly pink bathroom: that woman was no longer an enemy, but a sister in Christ. I was thankful that God had taken my heart of blistering unforgiveness and healed it with the soothing dew of rest.

Most times the only way to achieve the emotional balance needed for authentic rest is by working through ingrained patterns of thoughts and emotions. These patterns must be broken if we want to progress in the spiritual life. And permanently breaking those patterns involves forgiveness. We must forgive them. We must forgive God. We must forgive ourselves.

Isn't forgiving ourselves often the hardest part? What do we do when the memories and shame of our past rise to accuse us after Confession? First, recognize accusation as an attack of the enemy; accusation is not of God, who casts our sins "as far as the east is from the west" (Ps 103:12). Then, agree with the truth of it: *Yes, what I did was shameful. Yes, it was wrong. I am guilty of all my memory brings to mind, and all the enemy accuses me of, but I am forgiven. Therefore I forgive myself and rest in his love.* Say this, throw it all into the sea of forgiveness, and move on. Do it as many times as it takes, until it's complete. Stop giving your dominion of rest to the tormentors; live in the kingdom of God: confront the lies, acknowledge the truth, and move forward in freedom.

Forgiveness is the supreme task of justice. It doesn't mean what happened is okay, just that we are allowing God to make it right in us and them. We are trusting him with our emotions and with justice.

God began my great desert journey by allowing circumstances that provoked rebellion in other people around me, a predominant fault I shared with those people and that I had already worked with God to mitigate for considerable time. I judged the sin in my neighbor until God revealed the underlying wound and weakness in my own heart and led me to true forgiveness for both myself and them. But that wasn't the bottom of the wound. Nor was it the source of my ugliest eruptions. Not at all.

The Last Straw

I had spent a fruitless decade trying to get my Bible study published, a decade that ultimately culminated in my worst fears: total rejection. Although I consoled myself that the process had taught me how to formulate better queries, write effective proposals, create a website, build a platform, and find paying speaking engagements, with every rejection letter fear multiplied in my heart. After trumpeting my promise to all who would listen, failure seemed so huge and terrifying that I told no one. I had put so much pressure on myself to succeed—telling myself that God himself had *promised* I would one day be published—that with every rejection letter I felt like God had utterly rejected me as well. "Why won't you *help* me?!" I screamed at him, and with utter disgust I firmly resolved to finally quit wasting my time.

Over the next days he let me question his Word as I had understood it, he let me question my own sanity, and he sent dew through the scriptures to assure me, to encourage me to keep trying. I clung to Abraham, who waited *twenty-five* years, who stumbled and manipulated and questioned God repeatedly throughout, and who was assured of the veracity of his promise. After a month or so passed, I was just less angry enough to try again, only to receive another rejection.

It was my last. I dissolved in a tsunami of rage and tears and snot. A very deep and painful tear ripped through my soul, out of all proportion to the event. I raged and cursed at God. Just like the Israelites, I accused him of leading me around like a rutting bull by a nose ring, of bribing me with a carrot of promise, only to yank it back with ridicule just as I reached for it. My emotions were irrational, dangerous, and scary even to me. I pounded and wailed and screamed, "Why are you *doing* this to me?" My battles over negative thoughts and trusting God for superficial, daily needs had led me far into the back side of the desert and finally brought me to the end of myself, until the wound was fully raw and open.

He laid the answer on my heart gently: "I am doing this *for* you."

I scoffed. But in my (seemingly unrelated) scripture study at the time, a question drew itself up off the page in demand: *When was the first time you can remember feeling like this?* Startled, the dank caverns of my heart belched out memories like bloodsucking bats, painful reneges from childhood when my dad had made promises and then retracted them because of my behavior or some infraction by which he deemed me undeserving. The pain of what was under that last rejection stole my breath, and I gasped for air as my chest contracted.

After my parents divorced, my father did not show up for scheduled weekend visits several times a year. No phone call, no reason. Just left us sitting on the walkway, waiting for him. He would promise to pay for counseling and medical procedures, then leave me (over eighteen, but still a teenager making minimum wage) with the overwhelming expenses instead. I learned to always suspect ulterior motives. I learned never to trust what he promised. And that was why, I realized, I'd had such an irrational reaction regarding God's promise to me regarding publishing: I had been walking on eggshells, trying to make sure I didn't do anything to make God take it back.

I realized that in the pith of my soul where "worthlessness" lived, I *believed* I did not deserve such a promise from God, that I was unworthy of it. And it's true, I am of myself unworthy, but not by grace. With every rejection, I had punished myself with sabotaging negativity. I talked to myself in mean ways I would *never* use to speak to another person. I grasped that he had allowed with increasing intensity pop quiz after pop quiz, rejection after rejection, precisely to bring me to this awareness, this healing breaking point, just as he had the Israelites: "I am the LORD, your healer" (Ex 15:26). I understood he really was doing it *for* me, to a deeper end than I had ever fathomed or known I needed. This understanding settled gently over my scorched soul like the most bittersweet dew. I was deeply grateful, supremely ashamed of my accusations in the face of his goodness, and I quietened and stilled under the rejections and God's love for me there.

The Church calls such uncontrolled emotions and behaviors *disordered passions*, saying that "either man governs his passions and finds peace [rest], or he lets himself be dominated by them and becomes unhappy" (*CCC* 2339). The Bible puts it a little more coarsely: "Like a dog that returns to his vomit is a fool who repeats his folly" (Prv 26:11).

What is your emotional "vomit"? What destructive, disgusting behavior do you return to over and over, almost as second nature? How do I know you have emotional vomit? Because this verse refers to the vulgarity of sin, it applies to every sinner. What sin has so ensnared you that you fall into it without even considering the pattern or its root? Aren't you tired of repeating your folly?

Unresolved Anger Kills

Your emotional eruptions may not be rooted in a father wound. They will likely manifest differently than the rage I struggled with. But if you are like me and struggle with anger too, we are in pretty good company. Moses had a terrible temper, and ultimately it caused him to forfeit the promised land. He murdered a countryman, routinely grew exasperated with the Israelites, and threw the Ten Commandments down and broke them. The Word of God, y'all. Moses smashed the stone tablets written by the finger of God himself (Dt 9:10)!

Because of his uncontrolled anger, Moses could not rest in the promised land. Because of their uncontrolled fear, the Israelites could not rest in the promised land. And because of our uncontrolled emotions, God draws us into the desert too, to show us how to find the rest we need not just in our minds, but also in our emotions. Finding spiritual balance and healthy release of the stress and negative emotions that we encounter in our lives is rest.

Fast forward several thousand years to the New Testament, and the Hebrews are still struggling. The entire book of Hebrews was written to encourage them toward a particular type of emotional rest.

Let Go of Your Own Throat

Like so much of the New Testament, Hebrews is a pastoral epistle, a letter written to address a particular problem that arose in the early Church. The early Christians were mostly Jewish converts, and the letter to the Hebrews was written to dissuade them from returning to familiar old-covenant temple-worship practices. They were in danger of turning away from Christ, back to the perceived security of Judaism and the Old Testament Law: the letter of the law without the love of the Gospel. Yet "love does no wrong to a neighbor; therefore love is the fulfilling of the law" (Rom 13:10). What futility, to trade the fulfillment for its shadow. What tragedy, to turn away from freedom in love back to the strict rules and constrictive requirements of the law!

In some ways, it is perhaps understandable that, under vicious persecution, the early Christians were tempted to return to the comfort of the Jewish faith. Their homes, livelihoods, and even their lives were threatened by zealous Jews who felt Christians had committed apostasy and hijacked their faith. The letter to the Hebrews therefore details the superiority of Jesus' eternal sacrifice as high priest of the new covenant over the offerings of the old. It holds forth the idea that progressing in the freedom and love of Christian faith leads to rest, while returning to the rules, ceremonies, and traditions (works) of the Mosaic Law leads one to forfeit that rest.

Yet rules are comforting, are they not? They're easy to check off a list, simple to measure, manageable, comfortable, familiar. Holiness? Not so measurable or comfortable. Especially when you're talking about bringing rest to thoughts and emotions.

Most Catholics are not in danger of turning away from Christ to Judaism, but a great many of us are in danger of forfeiting rest to the superficial comfort of legalistic rule-keeping. Even St. Paul had his own struggles in this area, and so in the seventh chapter of Romans he spoke from personal experience about the tendency to stay stuck in (or reverting to) spiritual perfectionism or legalistic control as a no-fail recipe for unrest.

Is this something with which you struggle?

Perhaps the most common criticism I hear here in the South from non-Catholics about Catholicism is the accusation of "legalism," where our faith is perceived to be based in good works rather than the grace of Christ. They point to the fact that we have specific prayers for each day of the week and every possible need, Sunday and holy day "obligations," feasts for every month, liturgical rubrics, a magisterium, and an enormous body of canon law. In reality, these dogmatic, ecclesial, and liturgical norms are essential for the unity Christ desired for his universal (catholic) Church and help us through this desert "valley of tears" to the eternal promised land, and yet . . . perhaps there is also some truth to the allegation that we sometimes cling to the letter of the law without the love of the Gospel.

Legalism is an emotional strangler. We don't call it legalism anymore, mostly scrupulosity or pharisaism. But it makes us try to earn things from God, such as rest, by offering all the right prayers and practices and good deeds—when in reality God gifts these things to us, his beloved children. For instance, we may be interested in whether the Rosary is really the "most powerful prayer" because we want our prayer answered. But the power behind that prayer, and any prayer, is God himself. See how focusing on the "right" prayer or the "best" prayer to get what we want comes from earning rather than love? What if we simply spoke from the heart instead?

Scrupulous rule-keepers are frequently hypercritical and judgmental of themselves and others. Often they appear holy without *being* holy, those "whitewashed tombs" Jesus spoke about (Mt 23:27), in which all the "right" actions on the outside conceal hearts of putrid emotion on the inside. Spiritual perfectionism is rooted in such emotion, and when out of control, it can be deadly.

Martin Luther Had a Father Wound

As I wandered my great desert in the wake of repeated church splits, I began to explore the claims of the Catholic Church and felt compelled to research the reasons Martin Luther and those that came after him in the "Reformation" left in the first place.

I suspected the legitimacy of their actions, given all God had taught me about proper biblical submission to authority in my own life through my father, husband, pastors, and employers. I also had the larger context of the double-church splits in my own local church to confirm those lessons. Still, I held out hope that something about Luther's rebellion against the Catholic hierarchy was justified. My entire religious upbringing and life to that point depended on it!

Because I have homeschooled my boys to read from primary sources whenever possible, I searched out Martin Luther in his own words. I read his writings (translated from German) and biographies, notably *Young Man Luther* by Erik Erikson,[1] and I began to understand the reasons behind arguably the worst Church split in Christian history.

Erikson relates that Luther suffered severe emotional and physical abuse and trauma at the hands of parents and instructors, particularly his alcoholic father.[2] He later struggled with rage, depression, and despair.[3] After a terrifying "Saul" experience in a thunderstorm, Luther fled to the monastery and became a priest to escape his parents.[4]

As so often happens (see also *CCC* 2779), Luther's view of
God was framed by the anxiety and fear he felt toward his own
parents, particularly his father. Even as a priest, Luther suffered
from debilitating perfectionism, anxiety, and depression over
thoughts of God's harsh judgment for his own minute sins, which
he repeatedly confessed without assurance of forgiveness.

A gifted teacher and preacher, Luther was assigned numerous preaching and spiritual formation duties for others at the
monastery in addition to his extensive work, prayer, and worship
responsibilities under the Augustinian rule of his order. At some
point, he began skipping parts of the required fixed-hour prayer
of his order so that he could fit in all his responsibilities. Haunted
by lifelong insecurities about his salvation and standing with God,
the neglect of prayer led to deeper anxiety and struggles with perfectionism, and he became obsessed with catching up, sometimes
cramming hours of prayers late into the night, only to do it all
again the following day.

Realizing he could never compensate for all he had felt forced
to omit, and feeling he could never do enough to satisfy God,
he finally succumbed to despair and breakdown,[5] resolving that
"good works" were ultimately worthless. Luther needed relief
from works altogether since the impossibility of measuring up
plagued him so unmercifully, so he began to conflate the works
of the Mosaic Law with New Testament works. The first are legit-
imately obsolete (Heb 8:13); the second are absolutely necessary
for salvation and faith (Jas 2:14 ff).

Clinging selectively to favored biblical passages, Luther
developed beliefs and teachings about "salvation by faith *alone*"
that directly conflicted with both the Bible and historical teachings of the Catholic Church. For example, Luther used Romans
3:28 ("For we hold that a man is justified by faith apart from
works of law") to bolster his position that *all* works (not just the
ceremonial law of the Old Testament) are worthless and unnec-
essary. Yet he ignored other passages entirely, such as, "You see
that a man is justified by works and not by faith alone" (Jas 2:24).
Luther went so far as to purposely mistranslate or completely

remove texts to suit his new teachings, such as inserting "alone" in Romans 3:28: "For we hold that a man is justified by faith *alone* apart from works of law," defending this insertion with cursing and swearing. And Martin Luther is why there are seven fewer books in Protestant Bibles than Catholic Bibles.

While most contemporary Protestant translations no longer retain Luther's "alone" in Romans 3:28, Protestantism as a philosophy does. *Sola scriptura* and *sola fide* (scripture alone and faith alone) are the cry and foundation of Protestant doctrine and faith, and what followed was certainly no reform of the historical Church, but a splintering into sectarianism and division that Jesus, the apostles, and the Church Fathers all categorically denounce (Jn 17:17–23; 1 Cor 1:10–17, 3:1–4; Ti 3:9–11).

As the guardian of the deposit of faith (1 Tm 3:16), the Catholic bishops defended the Church against the errors of Luther's new teachings, but correction simply made Luther all the more intractable. His public denunciation of the hypocrisy and carnality he had witnessed in Rome necessarily exacerbated the conflict. You can almost feel the seething emotion in his writings at that time, and given the blatant sin of the Church hierarchy, one can sympathize with it.

Several biographers, but Erikson particularly, put forth that Luther was driven by spiritual perfectionism—mental, emotional, and spiritual imbalance rooted in childhood wounds.[6] Even before I read his biographies, as I read Luther's own words I clearly saw a man who was enslaved to out-of-control emotion that led to circular thoughts and toxic habits of spiritual rule-keeping. I saw a man who was angry and unholy; I heard his ugly tone; I recognized his rebellion; I could not believe he called the pope an ass![7]

Was Luther justified in his rebellion against the Church? Neither institutional scandal nor the infidelity of individuals in the hierarchy nullify the faithfulness and purposes of God in and through religious authority (Rom 3:3–4; Mt 8:5–13). Jesus never mounted a rebellion against the Jews or the Romans. He knew both were fulfilling God's purposes, and that God's judgment would occur at the proper time. Jesus simply witnessed to the truth, accepting the deadly consequences. He waited for God's deliverance, judgment, and reform, which swiftly came in AD 70 with the complete destruction of the Temple.

If only Martin Luther had followed this path, as did so many great saints such as Teresa of Avila and John of the Cross! Instead, he deliberately and presumptuously taught "strange doctrines" in an unconscious effort to soothe his own spiritual perfectionism, even after the Church corrected him. Although Luther had valid concerns about sin in the hierarchy, I recognized in his short temper, defiant attitude, erratic behavior, contradictory positions, ugly language, and astounding lack of holiness or humility a father wound similar to my own, causing him to act out in exactly the same ways I had for years. I could have been Martin Luther's little sister.

I too experienced childhood trauma and weeks of silent treatment that left me with anxiety and fear of my father. I too transferred my fear and anxiety from my father to our heavenly Father. Fear of criticism made me an obsessive-compulsive perfectionist, trying to satisfy God in all my actions. I too interpreted failure and pain as condemnation and punishment and saw every criticism and correction (especially from male superiors) as an attempt to control, manipulate, and force me into submission, an attack to be feared and resisted at all costs. I was militant and hostile when triggered, but underneath, I too was a child quivering in fear. In reading Luther's own words, I recognized the misery of spiritual perfectionism and rebellion, and its rotten fruit of division, the sin of Satan.

Are You a Perfectionist Judge?

Perfectionism is a no-fail recipe for unrest. It makes faith a panicky, perpetual, exhausting report card with an eternal GPA. Psychologists tell us that perfectionism is driven primarily by internal pressures, such as the desire to avoid failure or criticism, feelings of unworthiness, low self-esteem, and adverse childhood experiences.[8] It is frequently accompanied by depression, anxiety, addiction, obsessive-compulsive disorder, eating disorders, and even suicidal impulses.

Perfectionists set unrealistically high expectations for themselves and others, often because such standards were set for them by an overly critical, demanding authority figure. They are quick to find fault and minutely critical of mistakes, tend to procrastinate out of fear of failure, and often attempt to gain approval and validation from a specific authority figure in their lives, such as a parent.

Matthew 5:48 urges us to "be perfect, as your heavenly Father is perfect." There was a time when I interpreted this verse literally and floundered under the obscene pressure, believing the Bible meant that perfection is somehow expected and attainable through human effort. It wasn't until I discovered the scriptural meaning of the word *perfect* that I began to understand that my goal is not flawlessness, but spiritual maturity. The procrastination, tendency to avoid challenges, hypercriticism, and rigid all-or-nothing thinking of perfectionism is emotional slavery.

In my desert, I had discerned in my own perfectionism a kind of backwards pride that was rooted in my own father wound. Unlike Martin Luther, who pursued his rebellion to its divisive end, I had begun to trust God's love and saw the cruelty and self-punishment of perfectionism, a cruelty at odds with what I had been experiencing of God. I recognized that I had somehow strayed onto a path that had no heart. I saw in my local church the rotten fruit of Luther's "faith without works" philosophy as rebellious church members sinned blatantly and freely without any expectation of consequences, because "Jesus paid it all." And I saw all too clearly the hypocrisy of those who stood in front of the church after it had been irreparably broken and proclaimed themselves forgiven, without ever actually asking anyone for forgiveness.

Before me I had the clear examples of my own rebellious decade, two church splits, and Martin Luther's tortured view of God. All these things created in me a deeper hunger for truth, and I began to explore Catholicism as the root of Christianity, having seen how Luther's inability to trust God's love had caused him to diverge from biblical truth.

I offer the example of Luther not to "spike the ball" over the rightness of Catholicism but to point out how the emotional roots of spiritual perfectionism lead to deep unrest and destruction. St. Paul expressed this perfectly in his own bewilderment at the impossibility of keeping all the rules: "For I do not do what I want, but I do the very thing I hate" (Rom 7:15). And he identifies with the misery of the prodigal's legalistic brother when he hears the Father say, "You are always with me, and all that is mine is yours" (Lk 15:31).

Believe it! All that is the Father's is yours!

As I left my splintered faith community behind and began to explore the Catholic Church in earnest, I realized that I was finding, not more rules, but the authority of a Father's love, the kind of love two giants of Christian history—Luther and St. Paul—struggled to find. Like them, and the Hebrews before, I embarked on a path through the desert in pursuit of that truth, but it was only when I found the path of love that I was able to relinquish my never-ending attempts to earn God's gifts by manipulating him into giving them to me by being good enough, and to stop becoming irrationally angry when I felt unable to do so.

Just knowing the root of my irrational thoughts and emotions was so helpful in achieving rest. I was not out of the desert, but surveying how far I had come showed me I had made a deep turn toward the promised land.

Dust in the Winds of Change

When we speak of desert experiences, they almost invariably involve unrestful, gnarly events and circumstances that toss us emotionally like dust in the wind. And so, when we find ourselves in the desert, the rest we are seeking is not merely physical: savage thoughts, barbaric emotions, and spiritual longings must all be addressed, healed, and made fruitful. They will probably involve our deepest, most secret fears, the ones that rage within us.

But when all of that turmoil is over, what remains is a continual blessed Sabbath in which passions no longer rule and nothing can disturb that wholly separate peace. There is a method to the madness, an order to the chaos, meaning in the wandering. There is a conscious love and light, a dew of heaven, that we can and *must* trust with an absolute, steel will.

What causes you to be unrestful? What feelings are provoked when you feel you or someone you love has been wronged, when you aren't treated fairly, when you experience circumstances beyond your control, when you don't have what you need or want, or when someone is getting away with something that is wrong?

Although I did not fully appreciate their significance at the time, as a Protestant I prayed two fervent prayers. The first was for a single spiritual leader. I didn't know it then, but I was praying for a pope. Ha! The second was a desperate desire to be closer to God. I begged, *Is there not some way we can be closer, Lord? I just want to be* closer. I meant physically, thinking it impossible. How could I have dreamed while I was in the throes of "dying" in the desert that he was answering my prayers, and that he was about to draw me into his Church and give me the greatest gift of my entire life, the Eucharist?

You often do not have, beloved, because you complain more than you humbly ask God for what you need and yearn (Jas 4:1–2). What is more, God uses these desert wanderings to give us the rest we do not know how to ask for, as we discover in the story of Job.

Job's Secret Fear

The book of Job offers an interesting illustration that, on the surface, may seem unrelated to the Israelites' wilderness wanderings, but it supports this important point: healing unresolved secret fears is the great invitation of the desert; God leads us there to expose our fears, then transform and heal them.

Job seemed to have lived a charmed life, and yet he also harbored a secret, nagging fear of his own: not *what if*, but *when* would disaster arrive? Then, in a single day, Job plummeted from the height of prosperity to the pit of despair. He lost all his children in a strong wind, his wealth in raids and fire, and his health in a wave of incurable, painful boils. No doubt in the throes of her own grief, his wife turned on him, telling him to curse God and die. Even his friends accused him of deserving all he suffered.

Abandoned by all with God nowhere to be found, Job sat in an ash pile and wailed, "For the thing that I fear comes upon me, and what I dread befalls me. I am not at ease, nor am I quiet" (Jb 3:25–26). No stoic demeanor in the face of anguish, Job was real. He asked why honestly, without the Israelites' suspicion and accusations, and he was offered something that changed him forever. What is left when we have lost everything dear: our livelihood, our health, our marriage, and our friends?

Throughout the remaining chapters, Job's friends attempt to convince him of hidden sin for all that has befallen him, yet we are told at the start of the narrative that Job was a righteous man and because of that was singled out for such suffering by the enemy. Throughout, Job maintains his innocence. In his deep misery and despair, Job is tormented by visions of evil personified in an overwhelming, unconquerable monster poised to devour him. At the bitterest end of himself, he questions God personally.

Only then does God speak.

Face-to-face, God reveals to Job the beginnings of the cosmos and its staggering breadth; the interconnectedness and unity of all things; creation's exquisite macro- and microscopic detail and diversity; the order of the stars and planets in space; the plan and purpose every creature occupies in the minute order of the universe; and the arc of history from dinosaurs to the final conquering of evil; and in the face of this vast wisdom, matchless power, terrifying omnipotence, and dare I say vision of limitless quantum reality, Job repents. *Of what?* you might think as you read the account. The narrative is clear that Job is innocent of any sin.

And yet Job confesses, "I have uttered what I did not understand, things too wonderful for me, which I did not know. . . . I had heard of you by the hearing of the ear, but now my eye sees you" (42:3).

My word, what did Job *see*?

Perhaps that is exactly what God longs for us to ask in our own lonely, desolate deserts—for the dew of heaven, to *see* through the fog of urgency and veil of fear what the Israelites would not, to desire to know as we are known, so that what was before a knowing by faith becomes, as Job puts it, a knowing by *experience*. God *showed himself* to Job in his abyss of loss, and Job proclaimed that all is well.

There are several mysteries in the book of Job that warrant meditation, but for our discussion I want to point out the wail that seems to come from Job's gut when disaster hit: "*For the thing that I fear comes upon me, and what I dread befalls me*" (3:25, emphasis added).

In the midst of his soaring prosperity, Job held a great secret fear in his heart. The narrative does not say precisely what that fear was, but certainly all of his losses on that single destructive day were part of it. There seems to be a hint of this fear in his intercessory practices on behalf of his children after periods of feasting and partying, where he sacrificed "early in the morning" "according to the number of them all" (Jb 1:5). Does terror for your own children plague you?

Hidden deep in his heart was a fear that stalked Job even while outwardly he enjoyed health and wealth and the love of an abundant family. Did Job dwell on that fear? Did he worry over it? Why would God allow Job to suffer the very thing he dreaded? Why does he allow it for any of us?

This type of fear constricts and suffocates the soul, so that we are unable to rest in our blessings however numerous or rich they are. Instead, we multiply diversions and search for entertainments, as did the Israelites, to distract us from the dread lurking behind all the ordinary moments. God's love is determined to reach all the way to the deepest secret soul, so we can rest there. I know what Job experienced in that soul-searing exchange with God, because after that last publisher's rejection letter I also face-planted with humble gratitude and awe before God's gentle insistence on exposing and healing my own secret fear: complete, utter abandonment.

I contend that each of us cherishes and suffers under a fear like this, one we are afraid to even name for fear the naming will give it power and bring it to being. But what if the resistance of that fear, its simmering ominously in our thoughts under the surface, our constant backward looking, is what brings it to being? What if dragging it out to the open under God's all-searching eye and consciously offering it to his light and love neutralizes its destructive potential?

This is why the saints talk about loving their suffering: they know it is not arbitrary; they know it serves a healing purpose in Christ that is first specific to them and therefore redemptive for the whole Church.

Redeeming Our Suffering

We often talk about suffering as though its sole purpose is to offer it up: *I am suffering so I can offer it up for my soul and the souls in purgatory.* It is true that we can and should offer up our sufferings in union with Christ's, since that's part of what makes them redemptive rather than simply painful. But perhaps it is truer that we should *cooperate* with the deeper message and purifying work God is attempting through them so that our inner Sabbath can also be released into the whole Church and world. No matter how many big or little sufferings we offer up, if we do not also allow God to transform the thoughts and emotions surrounding our sufferings, we have not really discerned or submitted to their purpose—we have not undergone the deep transformation that Jesus died to give us and that the Bible calls a sabbath rest.

Because it is such a profound, secret work, only God can identify and accomplish in us the deep soul work of purgatory, or sanctification, as thoroughly as we need it. He does not simply cover our sins with his blood, he scrubs out the deep, set-in wounds, "all unrighteousness." We can and must dispose ourselves to receive this rest, but it is always still a gift, one that God insistently offers us through the repeating circumstances and relationships that are meant to attract our attention and cooperation.

Just as he had with the uncooperative Israelites, God allowed the provoking of Job's unconscious fear in a dreadful desert to bring it to the surface for resolution and healing. Job experienced God's omnipotence, omniscience, and omnipresence in an over-whelming encounter that sustained him forever after. Job did not attract misfortune by voicing worries and lack of faith, as the Israelites did, but God allowed Satan to test Job at the point of his greatest fear so it would never lurk under the surface and terrorize him again. Job trained his thoughts on God as his fear material-ized, he searched for God with faith throughout his desert, and God revealed himself to Job in an encounter that also transformed Job's desert into rest and prosperity. Job is an example of what to do in the desert.

Although present the entire time, Job's worries were hidden, only spoken *after* he had received what he feared most, probably because he had never before clearly recognized they were there. Utter desolation forced Job to confront both his fear, and the Reality behind his fear, and in that confrontation he *chose* faith in God's goodness. He chose to ask why in sincerity, not accusation. Job experienced the dew of heaven in his extraordinary encounter with God and lived the remainder of his life in an inner Sabbath rest. I imagine Job was never afraid of anything ever again, after he knew and experienced infinite quantum possibility in God. His fear was completely redeemed. This rest is our inheritance and birthright as God's children.

Judgment Is the Root of All Negativity

We *can* govern our thoughts and passions and find rest. We *must* govern our thoughts and emotions in order to find rest. We learn to govern our thoughts and emotions by trusting God with them and allowing him to transform them. Thoughts have boundaries: we can simply stop thinking negative thoughts, focusing instead on truth, which causes them to dry up, and we can also allow God to transform those negative thoughts through his Word. But emotions do not have boundaries. They cannot be controlled or ignored or silenced; they must be acknowledged and transformed. Unaddressed emotion is what drives negativity and makes it circular and uncontrollable. God most often will not transform negative emotions if they are not acknowledged honestly, because he respects our free will.

Had the Israelites been self-aware of the underlying fear and pain of their memories of bondage, they might have found a remedy for their continual complaining and accusations. Self-knowledge would have helped them discern the emotion driving the knots of negative thoughts rooted in their memories of Egyptian slavery. And taking that negative emotion to God in prayer would have diffused and transformed it and led them directly into the rest they sought in the promised land.

If thoughts are sparks of energy, emotions are currents. Isn't being in close contact with some people for periods of time like living with a high-powered electric fence? Living in currents of negativity, whether your own or other people's, is exhausting and depressing. This is why positive thinking, cognitive therapy, and even continual Bible studies are not always enough to give us rest. Sometimes we hit a wall we are unable to get beyond because the wall is unresolved emotion. It's the emotion behind the thoughts that breeds and draws more negativity, judgment, and destruction, is it not?

The converse is also true, however. Kindness and love produce kindness and love. We reap what we sow, so emotions must be transformed in order for our thoughts to be healthy, and vice versa. In her book *Who Switched Off My Brain?*, Dr. Caroline Leaf explains that there are only two types of emotions, fear and love, both with their own biology.[9] All other emotions are simply variations of the two. Love is the healing power. "Perfect love casts out fear" (1 Jn 4:18). So how can we cooperate with the Holy Spirit in transforming our negative emotions?

Scientific studies have shown that visualization and art, prayer, and healing all occur in the same places in the brain; they produce similar brain-wave patterns and physiological changes.[10]

In fact, visualization, imagination, and reflection produce the same physical changes in the brain as actually performing the imagined processes.[11]

Split-brain research focuses on differences in function between the right and left sides of the brain. Neurology research has revealed that the body processes every experience and emotion as image first in the right brain, then interprets the experience and emotion as thoughts and words in the left brain. That is, the brain receives sensory information via right brain as emotion and image, then the left brain translates the emotion and image into thought. Science is showing us that imagery is the human body's primary form of emotional communication.

However, in transferring from right to left, from emotion to thought, something vital frequently gets lost in the brain's translation. The left side of the brain often betrays our true feelings by analyzing, categorizing, and judging every experience we have and the emotions we feel as good or bad, right or wrong, acceptable or unacceptable. This automatic evaluation reinterprets, alters, and sometimes denies difficult truths about what happened.

We all know emotionally distant, unavailable people. Maybe that's you. When you block emotions for years, you train your brain to say, "I will not feel this bad thing." You become an expert at not feeling, but your mind, soul, and body keep score in disease and out-of-control habits and emotions.[12] Instead, we should ask, "What is this emotion trying to tell me?"

The brain may busily analyze, rationalize, categorize, and judge every experience and emotion we feel, but the spirit is a persistent truth teller. It will command our attention one way or another. The heart does not think; it feels, and feelings are not logical or sensible. But they are *truth*: "If you continue in my word . . . you will know the truth, and the truth will make you free" (Jn 8:31–32). This is why positive thinking that denies or deflects underlying emotions will never dispose you to receive rest. The truth we receive from the Holy Spirit in the Word of God enables us to discard old thought patterns, negative beliefs, and attachments to pain and wounds that keep us in bondage to stress, anxiety, unforgiveness, and negativity from experiences and people. God wants us to accept our emotions, ugliness and all, to stop judging them, and to know who he is in all of them.

What Is Not Redeemed Is Reproduced

This is what my friend with the cancer scare discovered in her desert. After acknowledging the repetition in the mother-daughter relationships in her family and walking through the Israelites' experiences in the scriptures, she realized she had "stuffed" the difficult, painful emotion surrounding her relationship with her mother and cancer in the years after her mother's death. She had prayed for peace for years and finally gave up, thinking God did not want her to have peace. She had been to therapy. She had participated in Bible studies. She had a daily scripture practice. She had not found rest because her emotions had not yet been redeemed and transformed. Instead, they were reproducing themselves in her racing mind, terrified heart, and exhausted body. She believed she could never rest.

Finally, help came: I countered her negative thinking with the truth of God's Word. Rest is his promise! Jesus died to give us rest! As she opened her mind to that truth, I suggested a visualization tool that I thought would help her get beyond the judgments she had made about her very real, very deep pain and anger: judgments such as, *I shouldn't feel angry, my mother is dying; I can't talk about cancer, because my mother needs to fight; I can't be afraid, because it's selfish; I can't grieve right now—my family needs me to be strong; I won't think about cancer, because thinking about cancer might give me cancer.* Unresolved anger and fear of cancer had simmered within her for decades until these feelings overtook her. She couldn't even ask me to pray that she didn't have cancer, for fear of saying the word out loud.

The judgments we make about our true feelings silence them, but because they are energy, the emotions do not disappear. They explode outwardly, as in my case, or are turned inward instead, where they metastasize and cause mental, emotional, spiritual, and physical unrest. Gentle souls like my friend would never dream of releasing all that anger and fear on others, so they stuff it down where it eats away at their health and peace. The determination to be "nice" or "easy to get along with" does violence to a delicate part of themselves that is important and necessary and that must be acknowledged and allowed a voice. Visualization with the Holy Spirit gives voice to emotions that have been judged too wrong or dangerous to express and transforms them in his love.

See how merely psyching yourself up with positive thinking cannot work? Politely saying one thing and feeling another is so ingrained in us, we rarely notice we are doing it. But the human subconscious is insistent. Tension, agitation, depression, anxiety, restlessness, moodiness, and apathy tell the absolute truth.

People who live consistently in this type of inner conflict are often victims of disease and health issues that they may have never considered could have a spiritual root or component.[13] Not only does the left brain have difficulty separating and identifying emotions, but the words it uses to describe how these emotions feel are often loaded with judgment, so that we are only really in touch with our thoughts about an emotion, not the emotion itself. This conflict causes physiological and psychological stress. Condemnation damages: it is a product of the Fall, and that's why Jesus told us not to engage in it. If you can suspend condemnation of your circumstances and emotions in the desert, you might find an entirely different reality, just as Job did, just as my friend did.

Often, if we have little self-knowledge and awareness, we live in the left brain's judgmental interpretation of an experience as good or bad and what the meaning of the experience is based on that judgment. Going deeper into the right brain's imagery tells the full truth of our experiences and feelings, because judgment is not a right-brain function. Judgment causes conflict between the heart and head. The body responds to conflicting messages by releasing stress hormones that elevate blood pressure, disrupt metabolism, increase muscle tension, and depress immunity.

As we see through our focal passage in Hebrews, we begin with thoughts and go deeper to emotion, because quieting destructive thoughts driven by unconscious fear is what makes real rest possible. Freedom from out-of-control thoughts and emotions is the truest, deepest rest. It calms our minds and hearts; it allows us to trust; it leads us to the promised land of rest, Sabbath in body and soul.

Let's Review

Let's review how to find rest in our emotions.

- God wants to help me find permanent rest in my emotions.
- Negative thought patterns such as perfectionism often originate in woundedness.
- Emotional eruptions indicate where the Holy Spirit is working to help me rest. The root of emotional eruption patterns can usually be found in my first memory of the same feeling.
- God does not choose sides. He is not on my side against my enemy. He loves all he has created. Conflict is an invitation to self-knowledge and deeper relationship with God.
- Rest in my emotions involves forgiveness.
- Visualization can help me find the root of negative thoughts and emotions when verbalization does not.

An Invitation

About a year ago I was having difficulty writing. I've published six books now and have never just *not* been able to write. It was more than writer's block, but I could not put my finger on the problem and couldn't write my way through it. I skipped whole sections that simply would not come to me and wrote what drivel I could, trying to circle back later, but none of it came easily, and I hated what I did write.

The experience was so foreign that I started to panic as my deadline approached. My thoughts were a rat's nest of negativity and judgment; it was a monumental struggle not to procrastinate. My go-to negative self-talk is always, What is *wrong* with me? and I was beating myself half to death with it after every day's work.

Whenever I find myself in negative circular thinking that cannot be resolved with logic, scripture, or prayer, I know it is an emotional block; I learned this from a memoir I read one summer in which the author shared an experience she had in therapy for childhood trauma. Over a decade or more, she had made progress using the usual cognitive (verbal) therapies, but had hit a wall until her doctor tried visualization. Intrigued, I tried it, and was so blown away I have continued to use this visualization tool when I discern my mind is locked up and holding my spirit hostage.

Closing my eyes, I asked the Holy Spirit to help me as I searched my heart for a picture of my current writing situation. Immediately a hard, dry ball of mud came to mind. I could see its dimpled, uneven brownness and feel how hard it was in my mind, almost like it had been baked in the desert sun; it even smelled like dirt in my imagination. The picture's name was "Hard."

When I was sure the picture was complete, I asked the Holy Spirit for his perspective, his wisdom, in a transforming picture. Just as quickly, I saw in my mind the hard-packed ball of mud dissolve into a little pile of damp dirt, and a single green, leafy shoot grew out of it. Its name was "Grow."

The writing did not get easier, but the panic disappeared as I replaced the negativity with something loving and living, and as my focus changed to love, the rewrites came to life. I finished the book—the book you are holding in your hands right now—and met the deadline. I pray it helps others grow for a long time.

Whatever your thoughts are about therapy and emotions and healing as fluffy, granola, woohoo hippie things, science proves suppressing or denying emotion causes disease,[14] while visualization and prayer help recover balance, rest, and effectiveness. The sports industry has used the science behind visualization to transform negativity and enhance performance for athletes such as Tom Brady, Michael Jordan, and Kobe Bryant.[15]

Within the destructive cyclone of thoughts in our minds is an emotionally manic dervish driving the whirl. Because we are intelligent, emoting, spiritual, and physical beings made in our Creator's image, we have to take a whole-person approach to rest in order to reach it. Because emotion subconsciously drives all our worst thoughts and fears, visualization can be a much more accurate truth teller regarding our unrest than restrictive, condemning words. So suspend your suspicion and disbelief and try it. Let us pray.

Benediction—LOVE the Word

This is a visualization exercise.[16] You need privacy, about thirty minutes, a couple of blank sheets of paper, and a box of crayons or colored markers.

How to Visualize Negative Emotions or Issues

1) Take several deep breaths. Spend as long as you need to focus, getting what the saints call "recollected" (or interiorly still and quiet) and, as best you can, in touch with God.
2) Focus your thoughts and attention on the negative emotion or situation, major or minor, that you need help with or want to work through: a work situation, relationship problem, health issue, or some other source of negativity or stress. Imagine what it feels like in your body. What does your issue look like? What image or images come up? Is there a face, an object, a place? Do not judge the image. Trust whatever you see as being okay, and reach for the color or colors that best express what you see and how you feel.
3) On the first sheet of paper, transfer any image(s) that your negative emotion or circumstance brought to mind in the Holy Spirit's presence, using whichever color "feels" most appropriate. Take a few minutes to develop the image until you feel it is complete.
4) Give the drawing a title with as few words as possible.
5) Set aside the first piece of paper.
6) Remembering that you are in the Holy Spirit's presence, ask him for a better way to see your negative or stressful circumstance. Ask him for a transforming image. Sit quietly with him until an image surfaces. Trust whatever you see as being

okay, and reach for the color or colors that express what you
see and how you feel.

7) Draw the new image, taking time to develop it until you reach
   a stopping point and are satisfied.

8) Give the new image a title with as few words as possible.

9) When you are ready, place the images side by side, and notice:
   What are the differences you see in the two pictures? Is there
   a message for you in the drawings? What do the colors in
   each image mean? How does your second drawing offer a
   new way to interpret and respond to your unrest, negativity,
   or pain? Should you make changes? What are they? Can you
   list concrete steps to aid you in that change?

The process is not about art; your drawings may only be lines
and colors. Mine are usually just blots of color and stick figures.
The images come so subtly you will likely distrust them, but resist
that temptation and draw yourself back to the Holy Spirit's presence. You are attempting in both exercises to bypass left-brain
verbal thoughts, get in touch with the right-brain emotion-image
that surfaced in your spirit, and then let that image be transformed by the Holy Spirit.

When the mind and heart have found peace from rampant
thoughts and predatory negative emotions, the body and soul can
finally rest. Let's explore physical and spiritual dew.

Four

BODY AND SOUL AT REST

Emerging from the Desert

[The LORD said . . .] "Therefore the sons of Israel shall keep the sabbath, observing the sabbath throughout their generations, as a perpetual covenant. It is a sign for ever between me and the sons of Israel that in six days the LORD made heaven and earth, and on the seventh day he rested, and was refreshed."

—Exodus 31:16–17

Did you see that? "Rested and refreshed."

In the beginning, there was sabbath, because God knows what we need: we need rest. Rest is not a luxury; it is a spiritual discipline and gift.

Rest is a promise.

We dispose ourselves to receive God's promise of rest through disciplines that offer "dew"—God's renewing presence that leads us to the superabundance of rest even while we are still in the desert. With him, we train our thoughts, transform our emotions, and discipline our schedules to rest our souls and bodies every week by keeping sabbath.

In order to understand what the sabbath rest in our Hebrews text means for us today (you may want to review the Hebrews text at the front of this book), it is imperative that we understand what sabbath originally meant for the Jews: it was always the center of Jewish life.

When the Bible talks about sabbath, it is associated with creation, when God "worked" for six days and "rested" on the seventh. Keeping sabbath is one of the Ten Commandments. As such, sabbath "worship is inscribed in the order of creation" (*CCC* 347) and in natural law. Perhaps that is why one of the easiest ways we can experience God's beauty and generosity is by surrounding ourselves with the glories of nature: the smell of his breath in earth, fir, and pine swirling in the mists of a dense forest; the taste and smell of salty spray at coastal edge; the feeling of a snowflake dissolving on your face; the sheer size and scope of a night sky teeming with stars and aurora—does anything place your awareness more directly in the presence of God like these experiences?

Old Testament sages loved to write poetry about God's creation. Ancient peoples lived closer to nature than most of us today, and Jewish wisdom always used the term *creation* when referring to nature as an expression of faith. In Psalm 104, the poet uses a special "home-building" metaphor for creation, a metaphor that became part of the whole Jewish understanding of the cosmos. The seven days in which God created are significant because they speak of divine perfection or completion; because seven is associated with covenants or oaths (Ex 31:16), the seven days of creation were a type of "covenant making" and "temple building."

Creation is a temple or home for humanity. In giving himself to creation in a covenant on the seventh day, we understand that God was making a covenant with humanity and that God's Sabbath was a sign of that covenant. Later that covenant was formalized with the Jews in the Law as a permanent memorial and observance, to be observed "until creation passes away" (Mt 5:18). The earth is man's home and place of worship.

Time was also created for us, since I AM exists in an eternal moment. Places are made of time and matter, both creations of God. God transcends both time and matter as pure Spirit, so there is nothing physical of God to see, hear, or sense at all unless he makes himself felt or sensed. God created time for us, not for himself: "To God, all moments of time are present in their immediacy" (*CCC* 600). "That which is, already has been; that which is to be, already has been; and God seeks what has been driven away" (Eccl 3:15). "Driven away" means what is past. Past, present, and future are all one in him.

Sometimes it is said that time is God's way of stopping everything from happening at once. In question 10 of his *Summa*, St. Thomas Aquinas relates that time is imperfect because it measures change, and God is unchangeable. God exists everywhere—in every moment past, present, and future—in the single present moment of I AM. Physicist Raymond Chiao puts it this way: "Not only are all distant parts of the universe woven together throughout space, but also its future and its past are entangled throughout time, as if the universe were one seamless garment."[1]

God is in all times and places at once—he is omnipresent. "The Most High does not dwell in houses made with hands" (Acts 7:48). He can never be absent to anyone or anything, ever: "In him we live and move and have our being" (Acts 17:28). God is no time and yet present at all times, no space and yet present in all of space. No created time, thing, or place can contain him, so while Sabbath was God's (Ex 20:10), he created it for our rest, not his own.

In an exchange of gifts, God commanded his people to return the Sabbath back to him: "For this is a sign between me and you throughout your generations, that you may know that I, the LORD, sanctify you" (Ex 30:13). The term *sanctify* means to dedicate, set apart, make holy. Sabbath is supposed to be set apart as *different*. How so?

Remembrance was an important part of the Sabbath; it was inextricably linked to the Israelites' redemption from Egyptian slavery (see Deuteronomy 5:15) and was part of the ceremonial law of the Old Testament. But remembrance (or memorial) in Jewish thought was not simply a happy reminder; it was a re-participation in the historical event, a way of being present as the communion of God's people in the original Exodus from that time forward in Jewish history. After they entered the promised land, the Israelites continued to "remember" over a Sabbath meal that included special ritual prayers of thanksgiving along with a type of mini-Passover meal of bread and wine.[2]

The structure of our Sunday Mass is strikingly similar to Jewish Sabbath worship practices. In a sense, we have been re-participating in the desert experiences of God's people throughout our exploration of Hebrews 3 and 4. We re-participate with them in Sabbath keeping too, with similar (though not identical) practices: it is a time for remembrance, for family, and for a cessation of labor. Above all, it is a time of rest.

The first express mention of the Sabbath is found in Exodus 16:21–30, in connection with the giving of the manna. Remember that throughout the forty years our spiritual ancestors wandered in the desert, nourishing manna rained from heaven with the dew every day except Friday, on which a double portion fell for each person, so that everyone had more than enough for the holy day without having to work to gather it.

For the Israelites, Sabbath was from sundown on Friday night until sundown on Saturday night, after the pattern of creation: "Thus evening came, and morning followed—the first day" (Gn 1:5, NAB). This evening-to-morning way of timekeeping is reflected in the Church's celebration of the same Mass on Saturday evening (the Vigil Mass) *and* Sunday morning.

Sabbath was the basis of sacred time for the people, and it included a weekly gathering, offering, worship, and rest. Six days of work were followed by a day of worship-rest. Like concentric circles radiating from the center, all the other Old Testament feasts were expanded Sabbaths leading to the final Sabbath of time and history. Six years of work were followed by one year of worship-rest. Seven years of this pattern were followed by a jubilee year. Think of that. Every seventh year the people spent the entire year in Sabbath rest, a practice after which we model our sabbaticals (though ours are shorter, since most of us would never dare to go an entire year without working). Every fiftieth year was a year of jubilee; combined with the previous sabbatical year, the people spent two entire years living off the volunteer produce of the land without working it or storing from it. The land lay fallow, all slaves were released from servitude, all debts were forgiven, and no one worked. What rest! What trust must have been required to refrain from working for two years back-to-back!

The practices associated with proper Sabbath keeping were worship and rest for everyone in the community, including servants, strangers, and animals (Ex 20:10). If the people observed worship but not rest, they had not properly kept God's "sabbath of solemn rest" (Ex 31:15; Lv 25:4). The opposite is also true: if they rested, but did not worship, they had not "kept" Sabbath. So we see that worship and rest are inextricably linked in Sabbath keeping. Worship and rest are not opposites; they are a Sabbath whole, rest for body and soul.

From Sabbath to Sunday

Christians bring Sabbath observance forward, following Jesus, who fulfilled Sabbath in his person by rising from the dead. The apostles observed the Lord's day on Sunday, the day of Jesus' Resurrection. John the Apostle was the first to call it the Lord's day (Rv 1:10). A similar phrase appears in *The Teaching of the Twelve Apostles*, also known as the *Didache* (Gk., "teaching"), a work written toward the end of the first century, in which readers were instructed to gather on the Lord's day to break bread and to give thanks (*Didache* 14:1). A similar practice is presupposed in Acts 20:7.

The *Catechism* says, "Sunday, the 'Lord's Day,' is the principal day for the celebration of the Eucharist because it is the day of the Resurrection. It is the pre-eminent day of the liturgical assembly, the day of the Christian family, and the day of joy and rest from work. Sunday is 'the foundation and kernel of the whole liturgical year'" (*CCC* 1193). I love thinking of Sunday as the kernel of my weeks and years, the center of my time on earth.

In the Old Testament, Sabbath was a time set aside each week, every Saturday, for worship-rest: to recall God's provision, work, and rest in creation, and the people's rescue from Egyptian slavery. It was and is a way of keeping time with God, so to speak, although God created time and transcends it. God is always working and always at rest, simultaneously.

Jesus embraced creation as his workplace, yet he was always at rest. After healing on the Sabbath, "Jesus answered them, 'My Father is working still, and I am working'" (Jn 5:17). Jesus knows that God is always working, but always at rest—heart, soul, and mind, if we can imagine pure Spirit this way. Jesus works as God works and rests as God rests: simultaneously.

Our daily work continues this work of creation. God works through us, so that the primary location for our spiritual formation is the workplace, wherever it is. Sunday crowns our workweek, orienting us to what God is doing in and through us, rather than what we are doing. Sunday is a deliberate act of interference, an interruption of our workweek, a decree of no-work, so we can notice, attend, listen to, and assimilate the work of God, to orient our work in his work.

When we work, whether that's at home, at a place of employment, or at a church, we are mostly focused on what *we* want to accomplish. Even when working for God in ministry, we usually begin with an idea of what we want to do for God, rather than what he might want to do through us. Sabbath is meant to bring our focus back to God and the work he wants to do through us at our places of employment, in our homes, and at the marketplace. What is God creating through me and my work? On Sunday, as we anticipate a new workweek, we might ask, "What does the Holy Spirit want to create?"

When work is finished and is well done, nothing but rest remains. In six days God finished his work, surveyed it, and pronounced it "very good" (Gn 1:31). There was no flaw. It was without fault before him. Therefore, since God's work was done, and well done, at the close of the sixth day, "he rested on the seventh day from all his work which he had done" (Gn 2:2). He had no sad reflections, no regrets. His rest was not marred, as what we call rest so often is, by negativity and anxieties: *Tomorrow I have to go back to work;* or, *I wish I had done this task differently;* or, *I have so much to do this week.*

Not God. Every part of creation, even man, was perfect to the utmost of its potential, and God took delight in contemplating and blessing the work from which he rested because it was complete and perfect. This is the rest which he offers. It is not something he imposes, not a luxury at the end of a grueling workweek that we can arbitrarily dispense with, but dew: "The sabbath was made for man, not man for the sabbath" (Mk 2:27). "We who have believed enter that rest" (Heb 4:3).

How do we rest soul and body like this? Our rest is inextricably linked to worship, in which we surrender ourselves completely for two simple reasons: first, because it orients us in the present, and second, because it points to the even greater mysteries that are still in store for us.

Like the Israelites, we worship, but our worship liturgy "remembers" redemption not from Egypt, but from sin. We enter into a re-participation of our redemption on the Cross through the Mass. Every week, we are conscious that "in everything God works for good" (Rom 8:28). Our duties and work of the week past and the week to come are being woven into something beautiful, something meaningful, something important that could not exist were we not at work in the world with him.

With the gifts of money, bread, and wine that are brought to the altar, we offer our whole being and week's work in a self-donating union with Jesus' sacrifice. We receive Jesus' work in time on our behalf in the Eucharist. The two gifts, ours with his, mingle in one redeeming sacrifice to God in time. Like the Israelites, bread and wine are part of our Communion meal, but now in Christ we receive the Body and Blood of our Lord. We go forth to create something new to offer again the next week.

The Necessity of Formal Worship

In contemplating God as the Intelligence that imagined and spoke the cosmos into being and the Energy that underlies and *lives* in everything in the universe, it may be tempting to set aside formal religious practice as man-made and woefully inadequate and restrictive, worshiping God instead in creation or elsewhere, without "religion." If God can be experienced so powerfully in nature, and cannot be limited by time and place, why do we participate in formal, "man-made" religious practices? New Age "theology," as well as Eastern and other polytheistic, non-Christian religions, fall particularly into this trap by approaching God as an impersonal, dualistic good-evil force (perhaps referring to him as "nothingness" or saying that "all is god") rather than a Person with preferences. Even other monotheistic religions (Judaism, Islam), in rejecting the Trinity, miss the unique communion provided in his full, personal revelation in Christ and his Eucharist.

While it is true that because of our human limitations it is impossible to fully capture the ineffable mystery of God, and therefore our earthly worship is but a shadow of the heavenly reality, still we worship for one simple reason: God himself has revealed throughout scripture that he loves ritual, liturgy, priesthood, liturgical prayer and feasts, incense, hierarchy, and all the incomplete outward appointments of our faith. After all, one of the first things he commanded in the desert during the Exodus was that they should build the worship tabernacle using the plans he gave to Moses on Mount Sinai (see Exodus 25–31), plans that specifically included all such trappings. And in the book of Revelation, the heavenly tabernacle revealed to St. John also includes them (Rv 15:5–8).

Religious practice, however inadequate it remains as an expression of invisible mysteries, however limited its efficacy by individual and collective disposition, is God's preferred vehicle for drawing us most fully into his presence and into relationship with him. Worship is part of natural law; we lay it aside to our destruction. But we must worship the way God prescribes, the way that draws us into the closest possible relationship with him, in order to rest fully.

A Rest That Reaches the Soul

I've been a Christian my whole life, but just after I came into full communion with the Church at thirty-three years old, I ran into a friend who had known me well as a non-Catholic, but with whom I had lost contact after our church split. She searched my face, asking, "What happened to you?" We were chatting in the cookie aisle at the grocery store.

"What do you mean?" I murmured, rattled.

"I have never seen you this peaceful. You were always so intense. Something about you is completely changed."

In wonder, I told her about the Eucharist and my conversion, amazed my inner rest was *visible!*

As the prophets, gospels, epistles, and Revelation reveal (detailed in my book *Fulfilled*), the Catholic Mass is the *closest* religious observance we can possibly practice on earth to the worship in heaven, our final rest. As gripping as experiences in creation and elsewhere are, one does not directly receive his Creator into himself as nourishing eucharistic manna-dew in the forest, on the beach, or at the denominational church down the street. No other religion or church on the face of the earth retains all the liturgical elements specified by God himself for *fullness* of proper worship. It's not an insult to other faiths to state that fact; it's simply true that they lack a great deal of what God knows will draw us most completely into intimacy with him.

Even in Catholicism, worship is not about me, what I like, or what I prefer. It's about what God wants and has communicated to us about proper worship. And what God wants is always what is *best* for us. God does not need our worship. But he longs for union with us, and he knows our souls *need* formal liturgical worship. A human being who says he does not need formal worship or liturgical worship is like a blind man saying he doesn't need to see. He doesn't know what there *is* to see and can have no idea what he is missing. But what blind person wouldn't want to see if he could?

By calling us to worship, God has provided a means of direct communion with him, a foretaste of the full revelation we will experience in heaven. Rather than complain about the solemnity of the ritual, perhaps we should celebrate the inability of liturgy to fully apprehend the matchless power that upholds and permeates all things. Maybe we should embrace the necessity of merely *approaching* his mystery in the Mass, knowing he is uniquely present there, leading us to a final apprehension in which we lay aside all physical shadows and forms and know as we are known.

The word *liturgy* was foreign to me as a non-Catholic, but I learned that it comes from the Greek word *leitourgia*, meaning "a work of the people." In its broadest sense, liturgy simply means "a ritual for public worship." It is important to note, though, that liturgy in the Old Testament denoted God's presence. Liturgy, then, is not about style or preference but *presence*. Liturgy is God's way of sanctifying space and time. God gives us worship liturgy, so it is not according to self-expression, individual desire, or arbitrary wishes; we do not presume to invent or eliminate sacred liturgy for ourselves. Worship is not about what I want, what I like, or what I prefer. Instead, liturgy is prayer most fully in God's presence, an attitude of orientation toward God, of listening, sensing, and receiving God in time and creation as "holy other" in wonder and adoration.

Proper Sunday keeping involves the worship liturgy in the Mass, its own spiritual rest. But Sunday also involves rest from physical work. We look back at how God worked through us in the past week and anticipate how he will work through us in the week to come.

Relaxing the Body

Sabbath foreshadowed our Sunday worship-rest. As was true for the Israelites' Sabbath observance, after six days of work, we haven't worshiped if we haven't rested, and we haven't rested if we haven't worshiped. God calls us to "enter that rest" in order to attain the right relationship between worship and work, between *ora* and *labora*. This right relationship must be a matter of priority, as Sabbath is part of the natural law built into creation.

Recalling Jesus' work of the Cross, we can participate in that supreme work by receiving the Eucharist and by offering our own duties and labors in communion with his. Even if we must work on Sunday like our pastors do, Sunday worship-rest remains an obligation. We can set aside another day every week for relaxation.

Sunday replaces the Old Testament Sabbath by fulfilling the rhythm and spirit of God's command. It is similar to Sabbath, but not the same. Sabbath ceremonially commemorated the Exodus, the saving event of salvation history for the Israelites. Because there was no grace in it, their Sabbath worship-rest could not communicate the truer, spiritual rest we enjoy in, with, and through Christ.

Jesus is our rest. Our perpetual weekly Sunday observance includes rest, worship, and remembrance of God's saving actions on our behalf in Christ. Keeping a proper weekly Sunday helps prevent busyness, burnout, sickness, and exhaustion.

Proper Priorities

Most Christians, if asked the proper, biblical order of priorities, would probably say: God, worship, work, family, rest. In practice, the amount of time we give to each priority every week likely makes them more like this: work, family, God (if we pray daily), worship (if we go to church weekly or daily), rest (if we rest at all). If the amount of time you give to each were an indication, how do you order your life, even if you don't say so out loud?

I know, taking an inventory of how one *really* spends time is convicting. (I didn't even mention social media. Ha!) The good news is that evaluating proper priorities is not necessarily about how much time we spend doing this or that. It's about giving the *best* of ourselves in the right order. Giving the best of ourselves in the proper order is the simple definition of consecration, or setting apart.

Both creation and the Ten Commandments show us that worship-rest is a whole, a priority at the top of the list under only God himself, and should be practiced every week. Immediate family relationships are next in the order of commandments, then other relationships, which assume marketplace, workplace, and other daily pursuits. Even though six days are given to it, work is the *last* priority in the hierarchy of commandments! Tough news at the outset for those of us who love our work, maybe too much, but the single most important principle in learning to rest is that the best part, the first part—the unspoiled, unhurried, unharried part of each week and day, Sundays and mornings—of me must go to God every week and every day. We *begin* with worship-rest in his presence, every week, every day. Next, the family sheep are fed, herded, and petted. Then there's the other work to do.

You know those little pickup trucks that precede and follow wide loads on the highway, with their flags and flashing lights that warn you to make way for the wide load coming? Structuring your weeks and days this way is like a set of those trucks, or Moses's staff that parted the Red Sea, or the lead bird that breaks the head-wind for a flock of migrating geese. The entire crazy week and day take on a freedom and ease you can scarcely imagine. Why?

Because you have already consciously given the week and day wholly to God; you know you are working *with* him throughout each task and duty, even while not focusing directly on him; time seems miraculously multiplied and you manage to do far more in less time than you did before; you are confident you will get done everything necessary; you trust whatever does not get done can wait until tomorrow or, by some inscrutable Providence, will miraculously not need to be done at all. Yes, I'm serious. So was Haggai: "You have looked for much, and behold, it came to little; and when you brought it home, I blew it away. Why? says the LORD of hosts. Because of my house that lies in ruins, while you busy yourselves each with his own house. Therefore the heavens above you have *withheld the dew*, and the earth has withheld its produce. And I have called for a drought upon the land and the hills, upon the grain, the new wine, the oil, upon what the ground brings forth, upon men and cattle, and upon all their labors" (Hg 1:9–11, emphasis added).

If you are feeling parched, you might want to stop and con-sider whether you are properly maintaining God's first "house": "Do you not know that you are God's temple and that God's Spirit dwells in you?" (1 Cor 3:16). Properly prioritizing worship-rest is a kind of sacramental covenant keeping, an ongoing "house build-ing" of creation. There's dew in that weekly and daily worship-rest.

Is your desert drought due to a neglect of properly prioritizing worship-rest on a weekly and daily basis?

What would our lives be like, how would we feel in our skin, how would our health improve, how would we treat those we connect with every day, if our highest priority really were worship-rest? If our days and entire week were planned and executed with that priority in mind? I can tell you, the sheer weight of the subconscious pressure you carry on a constant basis would disappear. I know, because I tested the principle rigorously.

I took God at his Word in the most literal sense. At first, I only tried it for Sunday. I set out to make Sunday a more holy day, a day of rest for myself and my family. The first change I made was to put Sunday dinner in the Crock-Pot on Saturday night. I did that for several weeks, and because I'm an all-or-nothing kind of girl, I also immediately refused any work on Sunday. At first it was difficult, as so many undone chores remained. The laundry screamed at me. The dishes rolled their eyes. But I held firm and left it all until Monday. Which drove me nuts.

So I began thinking and working ahead. Today, I no longer enslave myself to the Saturday Crock-Pot, because I enjoy cooking for my family and sharing a meal with them on Sundays after church. But I do not do dishes. Actually I don't do dishes anyway, since my kids have done them since they were ten, but I don't make *them* do dishes on Sunday. No one works. No Sunday homework. No Sunday just-this-little-thing-for-Monday tasks.

We ride bikes. We take walks. We fly kites and play games. I call my mom. I take a nap and binge British TV on Amazon Prime. I do the preparing-for-Monday-freak-out on Friday and Saturday and ignore it Sunday night. It takes *discipline* at first—physical, spiritual, mental, emotional discipline—but once you and your family are disciplined and get the rhythm, it's heaven! You have an entire day of guilt-free leisure for your whole family, every week.

Although morning prayer at home is itself worship and therefore consecrates our day, about a year ago I felt the Holy Spirit stirring my heart to reconsider daily Mass. I did, and then remembered how early I would have to rise. I promptly determined I would decide later. But I pondered it.

My prayer life was languishing in semi-eternal dryness. Not terrible, just "meh," but rote: I prayed my Rosary to focus, then read the daily readings. I got insights regularly. The subtlety of the impressions almost detracted from them, but I knew he was there.

I understand seasons of dryness are normal, so I muddled through. For a week I found myself showing up to prayer each morning, saying to God, with a sigh and a bit of a spiritual eye-roll, the only thing I could muster in the seeming deadness of my daily prayer: "Here I am, Lord." It remained unsaid, but present, the silent question: "Where are *you*?"

That Sunday I received Communion, and as I knelt in my pew to pray, I heard the Lord say clearly, maybe with a smile, "Here I am, Sonja."

I bit my tongue trying not to laugh out loud at his cheekiness! Because I had experienced the astounding fruit of keeping a proper Sunday worship-rest, I considered it worth the risk to seriously re-prioritize my day this way too: God and worship-rest in the Mass first thing.

Now my "most favoritest" moment of every day is the moment when God kisses the world with "good morning." For decades I missed those stunning brief seconds. I started rising early to go to Mass, and the sweetness of these few moments has captivated me since, so that I'm up before dawn watching dewdrops fat with promise sparkle in the early light before they evaporate unseen. Heart wide open, I'm receiving daily manna with the dew. I worship-rest before I work, and my yoke becomes easy as Jesus and I share the load.

What rest are we missing because we're sleeping? What secret dew is God's great, open hand showering on me while I blearily, blindly rush through my to-do list? What little miracle awaits my simple attention to my neighbor, this day? What if a simple reordering of my priorities is the dew of refreshment I need?

God is not the taskmaster; we are. What a thoughtful provision Sabbath is every day, every week. There is dew in building my house with God. What a blessing.

Breaking the Sabbath

Over and over throughout the scriptures, when God's people allowed breaking Sabbath to creep in and become habit, they were re-enslaved. The book of Nehemiah is about a man who felt burdened to restore the city of God, Jerusalem, to its proper place of glory and honor after Babylon had razed it and taken the people captive about a hundred years before. That meant rebuilding the city, Solomon's Temple (God's house), and the wall around it.

Nehemiah 13:15–22 and 2 Chronicles 36:15–21 give us clarity on these events in Israel's history, revealing that their subjugation to Babylon was a direct result of their neglecting and profaning the Sabbath. To profane literally means "to treat with contempt, to defile, to make common use of."[3] By failing to be thankful for the gift of six days and continuing to work and trade on the seventh, they treated Sabbath as a typical day. In order to prevent their work on the wall and the city from falling into ruin again, Nehemiah shut and locked the gates, stationed guards, and threatened the inhabitants with bodily harm should they attempt to further profane the Lord's Sabbath with commerce (Neh 13:15–22)!

Nehemiah considers this principle so important that perhaps you should begin now. Start rebuilding your "temple" with proper Sunday worship-rest.

Remember that one of God's desert ways is repetition? Ezekiel, priest and prophet, specified three times it was because they defiled Sabbath that the people died in the desert outside the promised land (Ez 20). Three times Ezekiel says if man keeps Sabbath, he will *live* by it. In the Hebrew language of that time, there were no superlative adjectives: we say good, better, best, but when they expressed the superlative of something, they said x of x, as in Holy of Holies, King of kings, etc., or they repeated it three times, as in "holy, holy, holy is the LORD of hosts" (Is 6:3).

Ezekiel's repetition is a superlative emphasis on carefully observing the Sabbath worship-rest, and he uses it as a warning to his fellow exiles. God's Chosen People were deported to Babylon for seventy years, ten times the covenant number, seven. Ten signifies testimony, law, responsibility, and the completeness of order (think the Ten Commandments). Fr. John Hardon, S.J., says that any number multiplied by ten is the highest possible.[4] Altogether the numerical symbolism seems to communicate that the people had broken both commandment and covenant by profaning the Sabbath, and that they were under a type of forced Sabbath until the land had recovered the Sabbaths it had missed due to their greed. When we defile the Sabbath, we become slaves to the enemy; we keep the Sabbath and live by it *in the promised land.*

If giving the best of ourselves in the proper order is the simple definition of consecration (or setting apart), then profaning or defiling something is to make it ordinary. If Sabbath contained an inherent blessing by which its keepers "lived," then the opposite is also true. Like all sin does, neglecting the Sabbath brings its own inherent consequences and is itself a symptom of a larger spiritual problem. A willful Sabbath breaker was put to death (Nm 15:32–36). As Wisdom teaches, "One is punished by the very things by which he sins" (11:16). Failure to keep Sabbath properly led to compromise after compromise, until God's people were displaced from the land by their enemies.

How much of my self-medication, toxic-relationship cycles, chronic busyness, insomnia, dis-ease, and hyper-stress is due to compromising my Sundays? What if a great deal of my unrest is a direct result of profaning the Sabbath principle?

Written in natural law and preserved in the Ten Commandments is the mandate to give time to God. Sabbath is not a luxury; it is a spiritual discipline. Ignoring our inherent need for worship-rest is detrimental to our physical, mental, emotional, and spiritual health. What if small, simple changes to my schedule in a conscious effort to make Sundays more holy could bring about the deep rest I long for? What if it's really as simple as worshiping and relaxing with my family on Sundays with a heart full of thanksgiving and attention to God's goodness to me the week before?

Sabbath Blessings

The Sabbath is exalted as one of the most valuable institutions in Israel's life by the great prophets who faced the crises of the Assyrian and Babylonian exiles. Great promises are attached to faithful observance of the holy day. The seventh day was uniquely set apart and blessed (Gn 2:3), so the Sabbath contained an inherent blessing by which its keepers "lived." Ezekiel 20 especially emphasizes this point. Three times God repeats that he gifted the people with divine revelation through statutes and ordinances on Mount Sinai, and three times he stresses keeping the Sabbath, "by whose observance man shall live" (20:11, 13, 21). Man *lives* by keeping a proper Sabbath. Why? Because God *blessed* that day. Uniquely.

Sabbath keepers are blessed and promised unique blessings (Is 56). Their lives and efforts are fertile and prolific (vv. 4–5). They are joyful (v. 7). They are drawn into intimate communion with God (v. 7). Their offerings and sacrifices are accepted (v. 7). They experience freedom and purpose. Sabbath keepers *live* (Ez 20). If the children of Israel got a "double portion" of manna on the sixth day in anticipation of the seventh, why can't I?

During the entire period from their deliverance out of Egypt to their captivity in Babylon, the people of God were distinguished from the nations about them by their worship of God and the observance of his holy day. Proper Sabbath observance preserved them from idolatry as a perpetual reminder of God's constant creativity through them and his provision for them. Even when Jerusalem suffered under attacks from their Babylonian enemies, God assured his people through the prophet Jeremiah that if they would hallow the Sabbath day, they would prosper and rest, and the city would remain forever (Jer 17:25). This shows that the spiritual observance of the Sabbath was the supreme test of their right relationship to God. Sabbath was both the sign and the memorial of that creative power which is able to make all things good, the sign of that same creative power working to restore all things to himself.

As the work of redemption finds its highest expression in the Cross of Christ, Sunday becomes the sign of that redemptive work. Remembering the Sabbath to keep it holy through our observance on Sunday is our sign and memorial of deliverance from sin and unto the new creation, the final Sabbath rest, which has begun and now is.

Indeed, "in returning and rest you shall be saved; in quietness and in trust shall be your strength" (Is 30:15). "Repent therefore, and turn again, that your sins may be blotted out, that *times of refreshing* may come from the presence of the Lord" (Acts 3:19, emphasis added). Sabbath's rest is a blessing that will refresh us and draw us into the heart of God on our pilgrimage through the desert, and when we reach the final promised land, we will find it familiar indeed. Let the dew fall on your Sunday.

Letting Go

Right around the time that I finally began to understand that the pathway out of my particular desert was leading closer and closer to the Catholic Church, a friend related that my study was on the managing editor's desk of the publisher for our denomination and was being reviewed in committee. I scarcely dared believe it. *Why in the world* now?! I thought.

I had learned to trust God for provision in my needs. I was observing a Sabbath discipline and its fruits. I had surreptitiously read through the *Catechism;* the early ante-Nicene Fathers; encyclicals, documents, apologetics, and Martin Luther—I read until I knew Catholicism was true.

Ironically, it was my growing respect for the truth of Catholicism that would prohibit my first Bible study from being published with my denominational publisher, and that was agony for me to accept, as it was a promise from God that I *believed.*

At that point, I had a major dilemma: if I came into full communion with the Catholic Church, I would be saying good-bye to my promise just when it was as close as it had ever been to coming true. St. Josemaría Escrivá once said, "Listen closely, apostolic soul: that feeling which our Lord himself has placed in your heart is Christ's and Christ's alone."[5] I too firmly believe that one who knows his calling must do everything in his power to live up to it, yet I saw no way forward. Publishing a Baptist Bible study as a Catholic would have been untenable for both the publisher and me, yet I saw no women doing specifically what I do in the Catholic Church.

St. James says, "Whoever knows what is right to do and fails to do it, for him it is sin" (Jas 4:17). I felt that if I came into the Church I was sinning against my promise, and that if I did not I was sinning against the truth of Catholicism: an impossible rock and hard place.

Again, Abraham's experience was precious dew in my desperation, as he was asked to sacrifice Isaac, his promise, on the altar. That's how I saw it when I entered the Catholic Church and began leaving the harshest desert season of my life. On the outside, I had no inkling I was exiting the desert; in fact it seemed I was deeper than ever in sand. My greatest fear was realized; I did not reach my promise. I had sacrificed it by my own hand.

But oh, what realization dawned with the dewfall. I was crucified with Christ, and yet I lived. "And the life I now live . . . I live by faith" (Gal 2:20). The dew was so refreshing, so invigorating, so renewing, I was able to endure what came next in almost undisturbed rest.

Let's Review

Let's review how keeping Sabbath through a proper Sunday observance leads your body and soul to rest.

- Sabbath means rest.
- Sabbath is part of natural law; breaking the weekly Sabbath principle leads to spiritual and physical destruction.
- My soul rests in worship; my body is refreshed in rest.

- Sunday is a day of obligation, like the Old Testament Sabbath, that includes rest, worship, offerings, and the gathering of God's people.
- Catholic liturgical worship in the Mass is *the* unique participation in the heavenly sacrificial liturgy and Communion feast and the closest we can come on earth to the worship occurring outside of time and space in heaven.
- We worship to rest properly; we rest to worship properly.
- Our Sunday observance points us to heaven, in which we will ultimately worship in communion forever with Jesus in the final promised land of rest.
- We *live* in the closest possible relationship with God when our time is centered and ordered in him and his Church through worship-rest.

An Invitation

It wasn't until I began writing this chapter on Sabbath that I realized God had gifted me—courtesy of COVID—a sabbatical year. My travel had completely stopped, and I had been living and writing off of the "bumper crop" of the previous year. With amazement, I counted that this sabbatical year began exactly six years after I entered my promised land, just after I began a proper weekly Sunday observance. I truly rested for the whole year, and as I write, I shake my head in wonder at the lavish generosity of God over his children when they live in faith of his absolute love!

Try it yourself. You can never out-give God.

Benediction—LOVE the Word

L | Listen (Receive the Word.)

"You shall keep my sabbaths, for this is a sign between me and you throughout your generations" (Ex 31:13).

O | Observe (Observe your relationships and circumstances.)

What is the most significant statement or scripture you read in this chapter?

Do you desire refreshing from the Lord? In what area of your life do you need his rest?

How has God spoken to you in this chapter about how you treat Sundays and other holy days?

What steps can you take to make Sunday a more holy day, a day of rest for yourself and your family?

V | Verbalize (Pray through your thoughts and emotions.)

Lord, you have shown me that my primary challenge about Sunday obligation is . . .

Lord, I sense you calling me to a more restful, reverent Sunday. In all honesty, I am probably experiencing very little mental, emotional, and spiritual rest because I rest and worship so little on Sundays. One way I commit to making my Sundays more restful and worshipful is by . . .

E | Entrust (May it be done to me according to your word.)

Lord, I believe it is your desire to be present with me in all of my work and rest. Help me make your holy day more holy, especially by being faithful in gathering at church and giving my body and soul a Sunday. I commit my Sundays more carefully to you, and I thank you for the gift of rest. Amen.

Five

THE REST OF THE STORY

For we who have believed enter that rest.

—Hebrews 4:3

A simple way of thinking about grace is "treating people better than they deserve when it is in their best interest to do so." In the Bible, the word for divine love, *agape*, is sometimes also translated "grace," or "charity," as in the great love passage in 1 Corinthians 13. Love and grace always give what is not deserved. The Israelites did not *know* the grace of drawing on their literal connection to love, and for most of my life neither did I.

At its core, unrest—the Israelites' unrest, Job's unrest, St. Paul's unrest, Martin Luther's unrest, my unrest, your unrest—is a lack of knowing "this grace in which we stand" (Rom 5:2), who God is and who we are in God. This lack of trust produces panic in deprivation, erratic knots of dark confusing thoughts, destructive emotional eruptions, brutal schedules, and enslavement to earning love from others and from God. The Israelites and Martin Luther did not enter the promised land of rest; their thoughts and emotions were too volatile to trust and rest, and they clung to destruction to the end. But Abraham, Job, and Paul, and by grace I too, learned to love him back with our small, lost selves, with no conditions.

Don't look for unconditional love while holding a bag of conditions, beloved. Only faith sees and knows what is invisible and untouchable. Throw yourself with complete abandonment on the quantum reality of this love.

Love does not force. It invites, suggests, coaxes, and attracts, but never imposes. Martin Luther's relationship with his father, and my relationship with my father, imprinted an irrational, unreal standard of demand, control, and worthlessness on our souls. Perhaps you have a painful imprint of your own. For us, tireless, useless works attempted to satisfy a yawning abyss of lovelessness that was never satisfied, because the bar was always elevated just beyond our reach. So it is important to make a distinction between works of grace that we are made for and are necessary for rest (Eph 2:8–10; Phil 2:12) and the "works" Martin Luther loathed and St. Paul discourages (Gal 2:16).

My unrelenting efforts to get published, sure of my promise from God, were not the "good works" mentioned in the Bible. Good works proceed from love. I worked from fear. I worked to earn. I worked to obligate God into giving me what I wanted. When thwarted, my reactions revealed a fundamental belief instilled in me as a child that doing all the right things—praying the right prayers and doing the right deeds at the right times, in the right amounts—would automatically result in the realization of my promise. Unconsciously, I worked and believed and *expected* such payment for my works. My faith was in my works.

And *that* is why God never allowed me to reach the promise on my own.

Perhaps you have worked similarly to "get" rest and peace. There is a subtle difference between working and earning that sometimes only God can discern in our motives. We must work. The entire process of sanctification is a sweaty enterprise that requires every kind of exertion. The obedient, second-generation Israelites still had to labor and war for the promised land. Job relentlessly confronted his fears in God's presence when the specter of death threatened to swallow him whole. Abraham, father of faith, was a knife stroke away from sacrificing his son of promise before he experienced and *knew* that God's secret crucible had fully conformed him into the image of God the Father and thereby made him worthy of his promised land as the father of many. St. Paul ruthlessly battled the rule keeping of his original faith, beating back the pressure to perform in order to enter into the grace and love of the Gospel. I had to work, but I had to learn to work from love and grace, not from fear and earning. Just as God's works are always a self-donation of love, so my works had to be a self-donation of love for them to be truly, eternally fruitful.

The promised land of rest is God's gift to us all, but we still have to work at disposing ourselves to receive it. The difference is, we can never earn what is God's gift of grace. It is the subtle distinction between a wage and a reward, between force and love. We work in love's power at every step by drawing on him, as he is love.

God will not allow us to earn what is his gift. Not because he is mean or wants to prove his superiority or demean us or yank us around, but because earning a gift is *impossible*. The Israelites refused to enter the promised land out of fear, but when God allowed them to permanently forfeit their promise, they suddenly attempted to *take* the land. They attempted to *force* what God intended as gift (see Numbers 14). Taking the land was futile, while receiving it as gift would have been fruitful, as the next generation of Israelites proved.

In his mercy, God also allowed the repeated thwarting of my unconscious attempts to earn my promise until the dark, molten emotion in the wounds that drove me erupted to the surface. I was so angry that he would not help me. That nothing I did seemed to work. Did he not love me? Only then could I see it: my attempts to obligate him to me, to earn his love and his promise, just as I had always tried to do with my father. *I am not your dad, Sonja,* he said to me through my husband.

Only then could I bring the hurts to God for transformation, one by one. Only then could he reveal his love. Only then could I trust him with my needs and endure waiting for him to provide. Only then could I offer gratitude for that love back to him. Only then did I stop trying to *earn* my promise. I believed, I knew, he loved me, whether I ever received the promise or not. I loved him back. No conditions. I laid it all on the altar and walked into the Catholic Church.

And only then was there room in the desert emptiness for him to bring to me, freely and unconditionally, what I had believed for a decade.

A Public Revelation

I went public on a Saturday with my father wound tweaking; I desperately wanted the respect of the man I married but was terrified by the impending revelation I was about to make: I was going to a Catholic Mass. My face was hot and my heart pounded as I groped for a legitimate excuse to leave in late afternoon, on a Saturday, in a dress, without having to reveal the true reason, but there was no use in prolonging the agony. Unless somebody died and their funeral could be arranged in under three minutes, no excuse would fly. I might as well get it over with since I had already decided to do it, and "whoever knows what is right to do and fails to do it, for him it is sin" (Jas 4:17).

My husband was on his riding lawn mower when he saw me walking in his direction, so he pulled up and cut the motor with a quizzical expression.

"I'm going to Mass," I threw out like a dare, albeit a squeaky one.

He looked at me a long moment with distaste wrinkling his brow and then shot back, "What? Are you gonna be a little *Catholic* girl, now?"

I was mildly surprised he knew what a Mass was, but in that moment I decided to let my freak flag fly. You know when something leaps out of your mouth, and you appreciate its terrifying brilliance afterward? That's how I felt later, remembering my expression of (purely humble) rebuke: "Are you *persecuting* me?"

My satisfaction at his shocked Holy-Spirit-conviction face lasted only long enough for me to jump in the car and escape down the driveway. I drove the twenty miles to church in a cloud of doubt. *Too late now!* my mind accused. I was out.

Over the course of a year, I had surreptitiously read my way through the early Church Fathers, the *Catechism*, scores of encyclicals and council documents, and annals of apologetics material, attempting to integrate the teachings into my previous education and understanding. But that Saturday afternoon was the day the wasteland of my desert acquired a public howling.

Thereafter my husband and I couldn't "speak Catholic" without arguing. I continued dropping Sunday dinner in the Crock-Pot before attending Vigil Mass every Saturday, and then went to the Baptist church on Sunday to lend as much normalcy as possible to our family's reputation and Sunday routine.

Although they themselves had neglected to set foot in a church for a decade and a half, my parents lamented that I had turned my back on everything I had been taught. That same year we had begun homeschooling our first child, pulling him out of a morally and academically failing rural school. My parents were positive he would develop like the blind cavefish in underground rivers that evolved with no color or eyes.

So when they learned I had also become Catholic, well, what more evidence did they need that I was the brashly independent child? They threw out anti-Catholic questions that were really statements-thou-shalt-not-argue-with, as though I hadn't asked myself all those indignant questions and reassured myself with the ancient answers a hundred or more times already.

Most of my Baptist friends pretended not to see me at the grocery. My denominational almost-publisher dropped me, and I didn't blame them. Well-meaning coworkers—bless their hearts—likened me to Eve and chastised my husband for allowing me to lead our family to hell.

Adding to our trouble, the autumn I came into the Church I was postpartum; my oldest child had a devastating accident that almost killed him and left him an invalid for months; and my pastor brought me on staff as the paid religious education director, displacing two beloved, long-serving volunteers, to the horror of our entire parish. When a seminarian at the parish began stalking me (not stalking as in he thinks I'm cute, but stalking as in he hates my guts), his sudden removal seemed to solidify the parish's disgust for the upstart Protestant girl without a Catholic clue in her head.

Divine Intervention

Remembering the church splits and my instructions in the scriptures at the time, I knew what I needed to do. Previously, when I asked if I was supposed to just let nasty church members run roughshod over the church, hurt God's people, and turn them away from the faith, possibly to be lost forever, the Lord told me to be silent and pray for his intervention: "If any one sees his brother committing what is not a deadly sin, he will ask, and God will give him life for those whose sin is not deadly" (1 Jn 5:16).

So I resolved to remain soft, to never mention Catholicism to my family members, and to answer any questions put to me by others with gentleness. I didn't try to defend myself or convince my husband, or anyone else, of the truth. I simply began a full-on assault on heaven in prayer. I read and prayed with St. John of the Cross, my patron saint, and he suffered with me. I hid a green scapular under my husband's side of the bed.

Careful not to wear a flaming robe of martyrdom over the tension, every time I felt the anxiety of the division in our family—and it was excruciating to think I might be guilty of splitting my family the way those church members had split our church—I gave it to God again. He pointed me to Mary, who quietly obeyed God before a holy man who simply did not yet understand, and whose actions were not those of malice but of not having been drawn fully into the truth at the time she was living it. She assented fully before her family and neighbors, bearing their suspicion. Was Mary a doormat? Was she helpless? Or did she have heroic faith that quietly waited on God to defend her as she prayed in submission to his will?

Nothing happened or changed that I could see. But a couple of months later my son was praying the Rosary at the kitchen table for school. He looked at me with shock.

"Momma! God just told me something!"

I, like most, am skeptical when someone says such a thing. So I didn't look at him. "Hmmm? What did he say?"

"He told me I needed to be baptized!"

Luke was nine and had "gotten saved," or "asked Jesus into his heart," as is the Protestant way, about a year before, but was afraid to be baptized in the megachurch we attended after leaving the rebellious church to hide out and recover. He didn't want thousands of people watching him up on display in the enormous baptistry, and he was wary of drowning while being "forcibly" submerged in the water. I hadn't pressured him, so his abrupt statement surprised and worried me: if I had him baptized at the Catholic church he was attending with me, my husband might suspect I pressured him to do so. But then again, it could also be my answer.

"Where do you want to do it? At the Catholic church or the Baptist one?"

When he indicated his desire for our priest to baptize him, my happiness was tempered equally with apprehension. "Well, *you* will have to tell your dad."

Three months later my husband witnessed his baptism, and our newborn son's, into the Catholic Church, with the tightest, most uncomfortable expression pasted on his face I've ever seen. But it was a twofer (that's "two-for-the-price-of-one" in Southern), and suddenly our family was Catholic three to one. And I hadn't contrived a thing.

Meanwhile the desert grit blew. My family pitied me; my friends shunned me; my enemies ridiculed me; my denomination abandoned me; my parish abhorred me; I feared divorce; I was caring for an invalid and a nursing infant; and I held a part-time job serving a parish that despised me, all while battling postpartum hormones. I clung to daily assurance in the scriptures that Mary was my model and that I was exactly where God wanted me through all of it. She encouraged me to be silent and soft, to refrain from defending myself, and to wait for God's vindication.

Months later, my husband and I were taking our customary Sunday afternoon walk together. I felt sorry for the tension between us and the fear and embarrassment he was enduring. I didn't look at him when I said, "You know, honey, you remind me of Joseph."

He stopped in the middle of the street and looked at me with shock. "What did you say?"

"You remind me of Joseph?" I repeated, unsure if I should.

"You're not going to believe what happened to me this morning." He meant while the kids and I were at Mass, since he had stopped going to church altogether. He went on with gathering excitement.

"I was sitting on the john this morning and God said to me, plain as day, 'You are Joseph.'"

It was my turn to be shocked. That was the second of several interventions that the Lord worked on my behalf with those who had judged me so painfully. The first was after I had secured evidence and our bishop had removed the stalking seminarian. Having experienced two evangelical church rebellions, my husband witnessed how legitimate church authority is meant to operate.

Five years later I asked my husband to video the RCIA classes I had been teaching.[1] He knew what I was asking, and I knew he knew, but he agreed. He participated in every RCIA class that year and learned the biblical foundations for Catholicism. He entered the Church the next Easter Vigil.

That spring, I questioned God about my promise. As a religious education director, I had seen the need for topical, Bible-based teaching in the Church for adults and had begun offering such. Was my promise really gone forever?

At Mass the readings were from Luke 13:6–9: "A man had a fig tree planted in his vineyard; and he came seeking fruit on it and found none. And he said to the vinedresser, 'Behold, these three years I have come seeking fruit on this fig tree, and I find none. Cut it down; why should it use up the ground?' And he answered him, 'Let it alone, sir, this year also, till I dig about it and put on manure. And if it bears fruit next year, well and good; but if not, you can cut it down.'"

I felt as though the Holy Spirit walked straight through me. A year later, almost exactly to the day, out of the blue, my first Catholic editor contacted me through Facebook about writing a book. And I hadn't contrived a thing! Now I am the Bible Study

Evangelista. Promise heard, promise understood, promise cherished, promise obeyed, promise loved, promise received as pure gift.

You too have a promise of real rest. There is grace in following God through the desert, the personal dew of heaven to experience in every need, an inner Sabbath to cultivate, and a promised land of soul-shattering love to live in and share with others you touch along the way.

The Rest Is Grace

Remember that dew was a symbol of grace in the Old Testament? Dew is dependable, while rain is less predictable, and dew is always a blessing, whereas rain can flood and damage, or arrive too early or too late for crops. Of rain and dew, the latter is considered the greater blessing in Jewish thought,[2] because rain was sometimes withheld when God's people had fallen into sin in order to correct and draw Israel back to him. But dew was a symbol of grace, God's constant goodness, unconditional on actions or behavior, the mercy that proceeds from his unceasing and immutable love for his children.

We are called to this rest, to experience and communicate it. Every person you are in contact with on a daily basis, whether closely or fleetingly, has the same desperate need for dew in the desert as you do. Because we are all connected by God's energy of love, even before you are living from it fully yourself, you can give a measure of rest to them by receiving it yourself. We are called to share this dew of rest.

Grace in Bloom

Aunt Betty was my husband's great-aunt. She was such an abrasive character, and yet oddly enough she was one of my greatest spiritual teachers. One month on my way to clean Aunt Betty's house, I pulled up to the drive-through just after dawn for breakfast, thinking about my morning reading from the great love chapter, 1 Corinthians 13. *How is love that "is not provoked" and "endures all things" even possible, Lord? Sheesh!*

I pulled up to the speaker, gave my order to the rudest woman awake, and coasted to the window to throw my money at her. Snatching for my purse in the seat beside me, I saw her notice the worn Bible resting there beside a cheerful bouquet of flowers I had hastily purchased for the crusty old woman I was headed to visit. I felt clearly that I should give my flowers to the uncivil woman in the window.

I balked. No one deserved them less. And what if my young son revealed I had given Aunt Betty's surprise flowers away to someone else? Still unwilling, I grabbed our breakfast and began to pull away when the impression to give her the flowers came again, more strongly. Because she had already turned, she never saw me *throw* the bouquet through the window at the last second.

But as I fled, I was also made to understand that phrase from 1 Corinthians in my morning reading: "[Love] is not provoked" (13:5 NKJV). I was made to understand that love is not a feeling, but a gift—a decision to treat others better than they deserve, just as the Lord has continually treated me.

Incredibly, upon my return to that drive-through a month later, the same irritable woman smiled and thanked me for making her day the month before. I couldn't believe she remembered. But it was I who was humbled by the bloom of grace.

Always Invite God into Your Needs

Experiencing need is not a sign of punishment; our deprivations safeguard us against an unhealthy sense of autonomy from God and from other people. We were created to need—to need God, to need one another. As the Lord said to St. Catherine of Siena in *The Dialogue*, "I could well have supplied each of you with all your needs, both spiritual and material. But I wanted to make you dependent on one another so that each of you would be my minister, dispensing the graces and gifts you have received from me."[3]

We cannot experience, nor communicate, God's grace as our provider unless we *need* something. Basic bodily needs, mental, emotional, and spiritual needs, are all invitations to experience him personally. It is a mistake to think the desert is preparing you to receive God in the promised land: you receive God in the desert, in the dew of heaven through every deprivation. He is already revealing his love in the desert as you trust him. The moment he provides for you is the moment you experience him. You enter the promised land having experienced that he is present with you in the desert, so that the desert itself *becomes* the promised land: "The desert shall rejoice and blossom" (Is 35:1). To struggle against the desert is to struggle against God himself.

Despite how scary it can feel for anyone battling unrest, even in dire circumstances we must never give in to fear, which Hebrews calls "evil unbelief." Humble risks can reap huge rewards in the spiritual life—fear prevents us from expressing our needs to God and experiencing the intimacy that comes from trust.

Think of how often Jesus expressed exasperation at the disciples' lack of faith, as in Mark 4, when he calmed the storm. They asked him if he did not care that they were perishing.

Where is the Lord's sensitivity for their anxiety, his compassion for their fear? How could he rest, asleep in the storm that was about to kill them all? What did Jesus know that we have not seemed to acclimate deeply in our own lives, as our lifeboats are tossed about by wave upon wave of real, relentless danger?

Jesus did not sympathize with his disciples' fear (then or now) because he knows fear comes from the enemy, and he loves us too much to let us languish in immature faith: "Perfect love casts out fear" (1 Jn 4:18). But among the lessons the disciples learned in that sinking boat was, surely, that Jesus is always working, but always at rest. Could they have set upon rowing vigorously during that storm, and still been at rest interiorly? I think so.

I've heard it said from Christians in the Holy Land that the stormy waters on the Sea of Galilee that day were a sign of God's power, present in Jesus, in the same way the Holy Spirit hovered over the agitated waters of primeval chaos in Genesis 1 to prepare it for life: "The earth was without form and void, and darkness was upon the face of the deep; and the Spirit of God was moving over the face of the waters" (Gn 1:2). Interestingly, the term "without form" is the same for "desert." The turmoil itself was a sign that

God was present in power, resting in the stern, yet preparing the storm to receive his word in a work of quantum order and rest. Jesus works in storms. Jesus rests in storms. Storms rest in Jesus. Even dust storms.

Choices, once executed, cannot be erased. Thoughts create faith, and faith creates everything. Thought is spiritual energy that once created can never be destroyed. Emotion drives thought and must be transformed in love to create life. You will use your faith-thoughts to make things happen. A word to the wise: be very careful what you allow yourself to ruminate over, because you can never determine the reality of a situation by simply looking at the circumstances. There is infinite possibility under the surface of what's visible.

Prayer, the Mass, Sundays, the scriptures, the sacraments—specifically the dew of the eucharistic manna—are what keep us resting in the awareness that all things are connected, in communion, with love as their essence. In prayer, including visualization, our thoughts contact quantum reality, or cosmic consciousness, higher thought, higher love. Your essence, the core of who you are, is God's light-love. You *are* love—you are *loved*.

Of all your earthly offerings, only love will remain at judgment; love is the only eternal reality (1 Cor 3:11–15). As the Lord told St. Catherine of Siena, "Each of you will be rewarded according to the measure of your love, not according to your work or time spent."[4] We must learn to love better and *more* in the desert, because our final promised land of rest will be the grace of what we created here, with love.

Love alone creates. Love affects and changes the universe.

Love redeemed the desert and made it fruitful. In the desert, you already have everything you need. Rest in what trust you have in him, no matter how small. All you have to do is ask, work in love, direct yourself toward, and wait for it with that littlest bit of trust. It all already exists in the desert with you, in him. The Israelites who died in the desert did not know this, but their experiences were left for us in the scriptures to reveal the way to that promised land, that Sabbath rest, the Dew of Heaven.

Rest Is a Person, the Dew of Heaven

You will never be satisfied to just know *about* God. Without calling it God, quantum theory suggests all things exist through, in, and with a "quantum nonlocality" that is outside of space and time and in which all possibilities exist simultaneously, as John's gospel puts it: "All things were made through him, and without him was not anything made that was made" (Jn 1:3).

One interpretation of quantum mechanics implies that a conscious Observer holds all things in being: "He is before all things, and in him all things hold together" (Col 1:17). As far as science has brought us in understanding God as the "force" all things exist in, there is a great mystery that science will never know and can never know, an immeasurable truth that had to be *revealed* because it cannot be discovered. A truth that brings this Observer infinite, radiating joy to show you and invite you into. And once we have entered into even the tiniest fraction of this infinite truth, we will radiate magnificence together, at each other, and at all else.

This Observer that holds you in an unbreakable and unbroken, searching observation is a Self, a Self as you are a self, a Self in relation with other selves: Father, Son, Holy Spirit; the God of Abraham, Isaac, Jacob, and you too. This Self exists to relate, to direct thought, emotion, and being from Itself. But this Self is also related to *you*. Your thoughts exist in this personal Self's awareness. Your emotions exist in this personal Self's awareness. All of your thoughts and emotions are related to everything else to which this personal Self is connected, which is everything.

No matter what the body that contains it looks like, when you meet a person, you know it's another person. A cat or dog is alive but is not a person. A flower or grass is alive, another life form, but not a *human* life form. Dolphins and chimpanzees push the line and feel "almost human" to us, but we know they are animals still. This Self is a Person as you are a person. You are a self, because it is a Self that made you as a part of Itself. It is personal. Being.

This Self is love (1 Jn 4:8). Selflessness.

Love, the *Power*.

"God is love" must surely be the most insufficient, soul-searing understatement known to humanity. And yet, how could words ever tell the full explosion of this truth?

How could the Big Bang contain the full potential of the universe in the second before it occurred? Archbishop Fulton Sheen framed it, "God could not keep, as it were, the secret of his Love—and the telling of it was Creation."[5] Science can measure the light that permeates all of creation, but it cannot reveal spiritual light and energy as a Self. Science can demonstrate forces, like gravity, but it cannot prove that the force of God's creative, sustaining power is *love*. Only the innumerable people who have experienced something of this overwhelming expanse of love can do that. They have told us. We must listen to them more closely. The Self is only love; it is only good. Creation is love manifested.

Powerful beyond all possible description, the warmest, strongest, gentlest, most expansive force in the universe, the generative love that holds in being all that is, created you and sends you forth as a piece of itself, its love. Is it strange to contemplate God in this way, to see him as so different from yourself, yet find that you're made from the same "stuff" of light and love? At your essence, you *are* love, the love of that Power. You are a loving self as he is a loving Self. He shows you the love in yourself, and he grows it there. This Self does not ask you to love him blindly, but to trust that he will reveal himself as love in your need. He longs with tender, true vulnerability for you to love him back like this, freely, unconditionally, to know him as deeply, and carefully, and intimately, and deliberately as you are known.

The mystics call this "union with God," and they speak of it in two ways that science shows us are actual. All things are *already* one with God by way of their beingness from God and in God. But working by faith—here a little, there a little (Is 28:10)—toward rest in our thoughts, emotions, body, and spirit unites our free will and participation incrementally in that unconditional love. We come to *know* this love for ourselves—we *see* this love as the essence of ourselves—and experience and live from and communicate it powerfully to other selves. We see others with respect for the spark of love that made them too. Faith is the engine of such discovery. This personal, Trinitarian love is what unifies and connects and *powers* the whole of everything.

Just as you are desperate to feel and know that loving Self, all things were also created, sent if you will, as a piece of that Self, and they long for love in the same searching, seeking, desperate way you do. This Love, who is the ultimate *Power*, loves at you every second in every breath. You *are*, and even that is an understatement. There is not a single moment that he is not directing respect and love at you; that is why you are *here*.

He sees you.

Imagine holding a caterpillar in your hand and bringing it up to your face. Do it, really: hold your hand in front of your face, closely. Now imagine seeing, not just a caterpillar, but a *Danaus plexippus* with one thousand four hundred twenty-two sensory hairs on its bright green 4.5 cm cylindrical body at the fifth instar larvae stage consisting of twelve segments with a complex banding pattern of one hundred forty-four dark brown stripes and forty eight white dots on its three pairs of true legs on the thorax and six pairs of short, fleshy prolegs on the abdomen and a head with six eyes peering up at you.

Now, be the caterpillar.

This all-knowing-all-searching-at-every-moment Self knows the self that is you this way. It knows and loves and *retains* every facet of your personality and temperament—every thought you've ever thought since birth to this second and unto your last breath; every explosive or passing emotion you've ever felt, conscious or unconscious; every intent and event and moment of your existence that makes you who you are—and he loves you for every single minute. Everything that defines you as yourself, unique from any other person or bit of creation, is visible and infinitely wonderful to him. He loves you so deeply and so intricately that he would never hurt you.

You do not love yourself when seeing yourself like this, do you? You feel the smallness, the confusion, the inadequacy, the darkness, the pain, the unforgiveness, the negativity. Yet he will teach you to love yourself without judgment, because he sees a piece of himself in your essence; he longs only for you to grow fully into being all he made you to be. That is all. In spirit and truth, he loves and wants you when you do not love or want yourself. He numbers "even the hairs of your head," but "fear not," he observes with love every one of them (Mt 10:30–31).

Your existence is enough. You are already held in love. The desert is meant to bring you back to yourself, to the you he made and sent from Love himself, so that you live an inner Sabbath with him that radiates in a warm circle to everyone and everything around you. The more you rest, the brighter your light and love become; with no deliberate effort you shine and warm all because you are connected to all. This is how peace on earth is spread—one brightly shining restful person at a time.

Depending on the translation you read from, several times in the Old Testament, as in Deuteronomy 33:13, the people of God are said to be blessed with the "dew of heaven." Elsewhere, this dew of heaven is said to be God's Word: "May my teaching drop as the rain, my speech distil as the dew" (Dt 32:2).

But in a touching and beautiful passage in Hosea, it seems it is not enough for God to drop the dew to refresh the earth overnight, nor enough to rain daily manna with the dew in the Eucharist, nor enough to send his Word to replenish our weary souls in the desert. No, your Creator must bend down his mighty face to peer directly into your eyes, he must reach down to *touch* you himself, personally, as the dew of heaven in the desert. "I will heal their faithlessness; I will love them freely, for my anger has turned from them. *I will be as the dew* to Israel" (Hos 14:4–5, emphasis added). The Church's liturgy picks up this touching imagery at her highest point of prayer, the second Eucharistic Prayer of the Mass: "Make holy, therefore, these gifts, we pray, by sending down your Spirit upon them like the dewfall. . . ."

When we enter the living "cell" of self-knowledge, as St. Catherine of Siena calls it, and attend to our unrestful thoughts, emotions, body, and soul, we can take them to Love in prayer.

Prayer taps into the Source of all being that connects all things and provides for all things. This attention, this observation, brings our wills, our hearts, our bodies, our minds, our emotions—our entire being—into an experienced reality in time and space of communion with the Dew of Heaven himself.

Supreme consciousness is Love, *the Power* that holds the universe together and connects everything that is. He is the Dew of Heaven, our eternal rest.

Let's Review

Let's review how to find rest in the desert.

- The desert is my mind, heart, body, and soul in unrest.
- Protracted unrest is unbelief.
- All possibility and provision exist in the desert.
- When I enter the desert, I can experience the Dew of Heaven in new and deeper ways.
- Emotion creates thought. Thought creates faith. Faith creates everything.
- The Word of God and the Eucharist are dew for my mind, heart, body, and soul.
- I have the mind of Christ (1 Cor 2:16). With the Holy Spirit's help and in his presence, I control my thoughts and acknowledge my emotions, without judgment.
- Controlling my thoughts involves seeing my circumstances from God's perspective through his Word (Jas 1:5). I should search for and thank him for the dew there.
- Controlling my emotions involves acknowledging and transforming with the Holy Spirit the truth of what I feel under my thoughts.
- When I worship-rest with the Church on Sundays, my soul and body rest.
- God himself is the dew that refreshes me in the desert.
- Rest is God. He is the Dew of Heaven, our inexhaustible rest.

- Thoughts at rest, emotions at rest, body and soul at rest—the self at rest in Rest himself—is inner Sabbath rest, the promised land of every child of God in Christ.

An Invitation

Like the Israelites' wretched subjugation in Egypt, every past spawns fierce and fiery thoughts and emotions that remain imprinted and reproduced until they are redeemed in love. The stunning truth is that the *deeper* essential imprint is love. This is the truth we must believe and trust with all our being. Our existence is this imprint, baptism embosses it more deeply, and the desert makes us one with that personal love, the love of the Trinity. Unbelievably, the Dew of Heaven makes himself vulnerable to us in the desert, revealing himself little by little in dewfall, drawing us into intimacy, seeking and longing for his love to be returned so that *we* imprint *him*: "Set me as a seal upon your heart, as a seal upon your arm; for love is strong as death" (Sg 8:6).

This is the love that made you.

This is the love you were made for.

Let us pray.

Benediction—LOVE the Word

L | Listen (Receive the Word.)

"Therefore, behold, I will allure her, and bring her into the wilderness, and speak tenderly to her" (Hos 2:14).

O | Observe (Observe your relationships and circumstances.)

If the desert is the soul in unrest, what is God saying to you about the Dew of Heaven through this verse, this book? What is the main truth God wants you to implement?

V | Verbalize (Pray through your thoughts and emotions.)

What do you want to say to him now?

E | Entrust (May it be done to me according to your word.)

Lord, I am ready to enter into that Sabbath rest. Lead me to dew in my desert. Speak to me, touch me, heal me, hold me. I am yours. I trust you with all that concerns me. Amen.

Notes

Introduction

1. The words "discipline" and "disciple" come from the same root.

2. Charles H. Spurgeon, "Grace Reviving Israel," The Spurgeon Library, accessed September 28, 2020, https://www.spurgeon.org/resource-library/sermons/grace-reviving-israel/#flipbook.

3. "The Blessing of Dew," One for Israel Ministry, last modified June 13, 2017, https://www.oneforisrael.org/bible-based-teaching-from-israel/the-blessing-of-dew.

4. "The Blessing of Dew," https://www.oneforisrael.org/bible-based-teaching-from-israel the-blessing-of-dew.

5. See https://biblestudyevangelista.com for LOVE the Word details, tutorials, free journal pages, teachings, and complete information.

One: Rest in the Wandering—God's Ways Are Desert Ways

1. James Swanson, "Desert," *Dictionary of Biblical Languages with Semantic Domains: Hebrew (Old Testament)* (Oak Harbor: Logos Research Systems, Inc., 1997).

2. John Paul II, "Letter to Reverend George V. Coyne, S.J., Director of the Vatican Observatory," Vatican, June 1, 1988, https://www.vatican.va/content/john-paul-ii/en/letters/1988/documents/hf_jp-ii_let_19880601_padre-coyne.html.

3. Don Lincoln, "What Is Inside an Atom Nucleus?" The Great Courses Daily, last modified August 10, 2020, https://www.thegreatcoursesdaily.com/what-is-inside-an-atom-nucleus/.

4. Raymond Chiao, "Quantum Nonlocalities: Experimental Evidence," in vol. 5 of *Quantum Mechanics: Scientific Perspectives on Divine Action,* ed. Robert J. Russell, Philip Clayton, Kirk Wegter-McNelly, and John Polkinghorne (Rome: Vatican Observatory, 2001), 22.

5. Fr. Richard Veras calls this connectedness "simultaneity." See "Simultaneity of the Sacraments," *Magnificat Magazine,* January 2021, 32.

6. John Paul II, "Letter to Reverend George V. Coyne, S.J., Director of the Vatican Observatory," https://www.vatican.va/content/john-paul-ii/en/letters/1988/documents/hf_jp-ii_let_19880601_padre-coyne.html.

7. Josemaría Escrivá, *The Way, the Forge, the Furrow* (New York: Scepter Publishers, 1939), 358.

8. You may want to make notes in the text itself, either here in the book or in your Bible. In my own Bible this passage is heavily noted and marked as I continue to return to the vital teaching in this passage and refer to its lessons on rest frequently.

9. Gregory the Great, "Book IV, Letter 31," Church Fathers, *Registrum Epistolarum,* New Advent, accessed September 2, 2020, https://www.newadvent.org/fathers/360204031.htm.

10. Teresa of Avila, *The Collected Works of St. Teresa of Avila,* vol. 3, trans. Kieran Kavanaugh, O.C.D., and Otilio Rodriguez, O.C.D. (Washington, DC: Washington Province of Discalced Carmelites, 1985), 386.

Two: Thoughts at Rest

1. Some scholars believe they are the same location, but others, after the Song of Moses (Dt 33:8), understand them to be separate places.

2. See Hebrews 3:9–10 in Bernard Orchard, ed., *Catholic Commentary on Holy Scripture* (New York: Thomas Nelson, 1953), accessed on Verbum software.

3. Mendel Kalmenson, "The Bitter Waters of Marah: You See What You Are," Chabad, last modified January 3, 2011, https://www.chabad.org/parshah/article_cdo/aid/1401655/jewish/The-Bitter-Waters-of-Marah-You-See-What-You-Are.htm.

4. Josephus, *Antiquities of the Jews,* 3.1.2.

5. "Bamidbar—Numbers—Chapter 11," Chabad, accessed September 28, 2020, https://www.chabad.org/library/bible_cdo/aid/9939/showrashi/true.

6. Josephus, *Antiquities,* 3.1.6.

7. See Sonja Corbitt, *Unleashed* (Notre Dame, IN: Ave Maria Press, 2015).

8. See Sonja Corbitt, *Fulfilled* (Westchester, PA: Ascension Press, 2018).

9. Caroline Leaf, *Who Switched Off My Brain?* (Southlake, TX: Thomas Nelson, 2009), 55.

10. Benedict XVI, "Mass for the Inauguration of the Pontificate," Vatican, April 24, 2005, https://www.vatican.va/content/benedict-xvi/en/homilies/2005/documents/hf_ben-xvi_hom_20050424_inizio-pontificato.html.

11. Fulton Sheen, *The Divine Romance* (Chicago: Biretta Books, 2014), 17.

12. Romans 11:8, which quotes Deuteronomy 29:4 and Isaiah 29:10 on the blindness, deafness, and stubbornness of Israel in the desert.

13. Leaf, *Who Switched Off My Brain?,* 61.

14. Quoted in Barbara Hagerty, "Prayer May Reshape Your Brain . . . and Your Reality," NPR, last modified May 20, 2009, https://www.npr.org/templates/story/story.php?storyId=104310443.

Three: Emotions at Rest

1. Erik Erikson studied with Anna Freud and remains one of psychology's most influential psychoanalysts. His stage theory expanded psychosocial research by exploring human development throughout life, including events of childhood, adulthood, and old age.

2. Erik H. Erikson, *Young Man Luther: A Study in Psychoanalysis and History* (New York: W. W. Norton, 1962), 29.

3. Francis J. McGarrigle, S.J., "The Psychoanalysis of Luther: Escape from Pessimism," *American Ecclesiastical Review* (March 1935): 252–70, accessed at CatholicCulture, www.catholicculture.org/culture/library/view.cfm?recnum=652.

4. Henry Ganss, "Martin Luther," *The Catholic Encyclopedia,* vol. 9 (New York: Robert Appleton Company, 1910), accessed at New Advent, last modified August 5, 2020, http://www.newadvent.org/cathen/09438b.htm.

5. Erikson, *Young Man Luther,* 27.

Four: Body and Soul at Rest

1. Chiao, "Quantum Nonlocalities," 22.

2. Jane E. Herman, "Blessings and Customs for Shabbat," ReformJudaism, https://reformjudaism.org/jewish-holidays/shabbat/blessings-and-customs-shabbat.

3. B. C. Birch and R. K. Harrison, "Profane," *The International Standard Bible Encyclopedia, Revised*, ed. Geoffrey W. Bromiley (Grand Rapids, MI: Wm. B. Eerdmans, 1979–1988).

4. John Hardon, S.J., *Modern Catholic Dictionary* (Bardstown, KY: Eternal Life, 1999), 382.

5. Escrivá, *Way*, 161.

Five: The Rest of the Story

1. To me it is beautifully ironic that I asked him to video the RCIA classes that I had been teaching for five years using a faith-formation curriculum that I wrote in order that I might submit the study to a publisher. Partially because of his willingness to help me, that study *was* later published as *Fulfilled: Uncovering the Biblical Foundations of Catholicism* and became a bestseller, and he entered the Church the next year.

2. "Blessing of Dew," One For Israel Ministry.

3. Catherine of Siena, *The Dialogue* (Mahwah, NJ: Paulist Press, 1980), 38.

4. Catherine of Siena, *Dialogue*, 357.

5. Sheen, *Divine Romance*, 17.

6. I should point out that Erikson was a supporter of the "Reformation" sparked l Luther's rebellion, so his analysis certainly was not intended to undermine its legitimac although in my mind that's exactly what it did, along with the similar conclusions others who share Erikson's opinions on Luther's emotional imbalance. There is tc much biblical exhortation against rebellion and division to defend the "Reformatioi in my view, even when confrontation and correction against authority are warrante as they certainly were in Luther's time and even our own. But the Bible gives us cle: directives on how to proceed in such cases, directives Luther was too emotional unstable to trust or follow.

7. Martin Luther, *Luther's Works*, vol. 41, *Church and Ministry III*, ed. Eric V Gritsch (Minneapolis: Fortress Press, 1966), 281.

8. Hara Estroff Marano, "Pitfalls of Perfectionism," *Psychology Today*, March 2008, www.psychologytoday.com/us/articles/200803/pitfalls-perfectionism.

9. Leaf, *Who Switched Off My Brain?*, 87.

10. Girija Kaimal, Kendra Ray, and Juan Muniz, "Reduction of Cortisol Lev els and Participants' Responses Following Art Making," *Journal of the America Art Therapy Association* 33, no. 2 (2016): 74–80, https://www.tandfonline.com/do full/10.1080/07421656.2016.1166832?journalCode=uart2; Rosalie R. Pratt, "Ar Dance, and Music Therapy," *Physical Medicine and Rehabilitation Clinics of Nort America* 15, no. 4 (2004): 827–41, https://pubmed.ncbi.nlm.nih.gov/15458755/; Haral J. Hamre, Claudia M. Witt, Anja Glockmann, Renatus Ziegler, Stefan N. Willich, an Helmut Kiene, "Anthroposophic Therapy for Chronic Depression: A Four-Year Pro spective Cohort Study," *BMC Psychiatry* 6, no. 1 (2006), https://pubmed.ncbi.nlm.nih gov/17173663/; Linda E. Carlson and Sheila N. Garland, "Impact of Mindfulness-Base(Stress Reduction (MBSR) on Sleep, Mood, Stress and Fatigue Symptoms in Cance Outpatients," *International Journal of Behavioral Medicine* 12, no. 4 (2005): 278–85 https://pubmed.ncbi.nlm.nih.gov/16262547/.

11. Jean Decety and Julie Grèzes, "The Power of Simulation: Imagining One'! Own and Other's Behavior," *Brain Research* 1079, no. 1 (2006): 4–14, https://www sciencedirect.com/science/article/abs/pii/S0006899306000102.

12. Bessel van der Kolk, *The Body Keeps the Score: Brain, Mind, and Body in th(Healing of Trauma* (New York: Penguin Books, 2014).

13. Cathy A. Malchiodi, *Handbook of Art Therapy*, 2nd ed. (New York: Guilford Press, 2012); see also Ohio University, "Dwelling on Stressful Events Can Increase Inflammation in the Body, Study Finds," ScienceDaily, March 13, 2013, https://www. sciencedaily.com/releases/2013/03/130313182255.htm; "E-Motion: How Your Emotional Baggage May Be Sabotaging Your Health, and What to Do About It," Mercola, last modified March 14, 2015, https://articles.mercola.com/sites/articles/ archive/2015/03/14/trapped-emotional-energy.aspx.

14. Malchiodi, *Handbook of Art Therapy*.

15. *The Last Dance*, directed by Jason Hehir (Scotts Valley, CA: Netflix, ESPN, 2020).

16. Adapted to specifically invite the Holy Spirit into the process, from Barbara Ganim, *Art and Healing: Using Expressive Art to Heal Your Body, Mind, and Spirit* (Brattleboro, VT: Echo Point Books and Media, 1999).

Sonja Corbitt is a Catholic author and speaker who has produced several multimedia Bible studies, including *Unleashed, Fearless,* and *Exalted.* She also created the LOVE the Word Bible study method.

Corbitt is the host of *Evangelista Bible Study* on CatholicTV and the *Bible Study Evangelista Show* on radio and podcast. She is in formation as a Third Order Carmelite. Corbitt is a columnist at *The Great Adventure Bible Study* blog and a contributor to *Magnificat.*

A Carolina native who was raised as a Southern Baptist, Corbitt attended Mitchell College and the Southern Baptist Seminary Extension before converting to Catholicism. She has since served as director of religious education at St. John Vianney Catholic Church in Gallatin, Tennessee, and as executive director of Risen Radio in Lebanon, Tennessee.

She lives in Tennessee with her husband, Bob, and their two sons.

biblestudyevangelista.com
Facebook: sonjacorbitt
Instagram: @biblestudyevangelista
Pinterest: bibleevangelista

MORE BOOKS BY
Sonja Corbitt

Unleashed
How to Receive Everything the Holy Spirt Wants to Give You

In *Unleashed*, Sonja Corbitt shows us through the Word of God
how the Holy Spirit is working and inviting us to cooperate with him in the patterns
of our relationships, circumstances, prayer, and times of suffering.

Fearless
Conquer Your Demons and Love with Abandon

Paralyzing emotions such as fear, stress, and anxiety can often be the direct result
of our everyday battles against sin and temptation. *Fearless* takes us deep into
scripture and the spiritual practices of the Church to combat these emotions and
equip us with the spiritual tools we need to restore our spiritual well-being.

Exalted
How the Power of the Magnificat Can Transform Us

Unlock the treasures contained within Mary's Magnificat, revealing a song
that speaks to each of us in a unique way, calling us to delight in the power
of God to transform us and making us into everything he created us to be so we
can revel in the fullness and joy of life in Christ with Mary.

**Find more resources from Sonja Corbitt
at biblestudyevangelista.com.**